THE WAY PEOPLE LIVE

Life in the Amazon Rain Forest

Titles in The Way People Live series include:

THE WAY
PEOPLE
LIVE

Life in the Amazon Rain Forest

by Stuart A. Kallen

Lucent Books, P.O. Box 289011, San Diego, CA 92198-9011

Library of Congress Cataloging-in-Publication Data

Kallen, Stuart A., 1955–
    Life in the Amazon rain forest / by Stuart A. Kallen.
       p.   cm. — (The way people live)
    Includes bibliographical references and index.
    Summary: Describes the history, life, and culture of the Yanomami, an
indigenous tribe still living a primitive existence in the Amazon rain forest.
    ISBN 1-56006-387-4 (lib. : alk. paper)
    1. Yanomami Indians—Juvenile literature.   2. Indians of South America
—Amazon River Region—Juvenile literature.   3. Human ecology—
Amazon River Region—Juvenile literature.   [1. Yanomami Indians.
2. Indians of South America—Amazon River Region.] I. Title.   II. Series.
F2520.1.Y3K35   1999
981'.100498—dc21   98-43616
                                                                                            CIP
                                                                                            AC

Copyright 1999 by Lucent Books, Inc., P.O. Box 289011, San Diego, California, 92198-9011

Printed in the U.S.A.

Contents

Discovering the Humanity in Us All

The Way People Live series focuses on pockets of human culture. Some of these are current cultures, like the Eskimos of the Arctic; others no longer exist, such as the Jewish ghetto in Warsaw during World War II. What many of these cultural pockets share, however, is the fact that they have been viewed before, but not completely understood.

To really understand any culture, it is necessary to strip the mind of the common notions we hold about groups of people. These stereotypes are the archenemies of learning. It does not even matter whether the stereotypes are positive or negative; they are confining and tight. Removing them is a challenge that's not easily met, as anyone who has ever tried it will admit. Ideas that do not fit into the templates we create are unwelcome visitors—ones we would prefer remain quietly in a corner or forgotten room.

The cowboy of the Old West is a good example of such confining roles. The cowboy was courageous, yet soft-spoken. His time (it is always a he, in our template) was spent alternatively saving a rancher's daughter from certain death on a runaway stagecoach, or shooting it out with rustlers. At times, of course, he was likely to get a little crazy in town after a trail drive, but for the most part, he was the epitome of inner strength. It is disconcerting to find out that the cowboy is human, even a bit childish. Can it really be true that cowboys would line up to help the cook on the trail drive grind coffee, just hoping he would give them a little stick of pep-

permint candy that came with the coffee shipment? The idea of tough cowboys vying with one another to help "Coosie" (as they called their cooks) for a bit of candy seems silly and out of place.

So is the vision of Eskimos playing video games and watching MTV, living in prefab housing in the Arctic. It just does not fit with what "Eskimo" means. We are far more comfortable with snow igloos and whale blubber, harpoons and kayaks.

Although the cultures dealt with in Lucent's The Way People Live series are often historically and socially well known, the emphasis is on the personal aspects of life. Groups of people, while unquestionably affected by their politics and their governmental structures, are more than those institutions. How do people in a particular time and place educate their children? What do they eat? And how do they build their houses? What kinds of work do they do? What kinds of games do they enjoy? The answers to these questions bring these cultures to life. People's lives are revealed in the particulars and only by knowing the particulars can we understand these cultures' will to survive and their moments of weakness and greatness.

This is not to say that understanding politics does not help to understand a culture. There is no question that the Warsaw ghetto, for example, was a culture that was brought about by the politics and social ideas of Adolf Hitler and the Third Reich. But the Jews who were crowded together in the ghetto cannot be understood by the Reich's politics. Their life was a day-to-day battle for existence, and the creativity and methods they used to prolong their lives is a vital story of human perseverance that would be denied by focusing only on the institutions of Hitler's Germany. Knowing that children as young as five or six outwitted Nazi guards on a daily basis, that Jewish policemen helped the Germans control the ghetto, that children attended secret schools in the ghetto and even earned diplomas—these are the things that reveal the fabric of life, that can inspire, intrigue, and amaze.

Books in The Way People Live series allow both the casual reader and the student to see humans as victims, heroes, and onlookers. And although humans act in ways that can fill us with feelings of sorrow and revulsion, it is important to remember that "hero," "predator," and "victim" are dangerous terms. Heaping undue pity or praise on people reduces them to objects, and strips them of their humanity.

Seeing the Jews of Warsaw only as victims is to deny their humanity. Seeing them only as they appear in surviving photos, staring at the camera with infinite sadness, is limiting, both to them and to those who want to understand them. To an object of pity, the only appropriate response becomes "Those poor creatures!" and that reduces both the quality of their struggle and the depth of their despair. No one is served by such two-dimensional views of people and their cultures.

With this in mind, The Way People Live series strives to flesh out the traditional, two-dimensional views of people in various cultures and historical circumstances. Using a wide variety of primary quotations—the words not only of the politicians and government leaders, but of the real people whose lives are being examined—each book in the series attempts to show an honest and complete picture of a culture removed from our own by time or space.

By examining cultures in this way, the reader will notice not only the glaring differences from his or her own culture, but also will be struck by the similarities. For indeed, people share common needs—warmth, good company, stability, and affirmation from others. Ultimately, seeing how people really live, or have lived can only enrich our understanding of ourselves.

The Threatened Natives of the Amazon

The Amazonian jungle is at once an immense, mighty rain forest and a fragile, dwindling woodland. It is the largest remaining wilderness area in the world, but an area the size of New Jersey is destroyed within Amazonia every year. There are hundreds of thousands of species of plants and animals there, including many that live nowhere else. But they are quickly being replaced by one species—humans. The natives of Amazonia have needs, abilities, and talents similar to those of other people. But they differ in the way their lives affect the forest and how the forest supports them.

The few remaining natives of the Amazon rain forest walk softly through the jungle and receive from it all of life's necessities. Today they are a vanishing minority among the rain forest peoples. Many more people who live in the forest participate in commerce. They fell millions of acres of trees with chain saws, they plant crops that may have come from the other side of the globe, and some even take their orders from people who have never seen the rain forest. Nevertheless, they, too, are people of the rain forest. They make their living from its resources, and their actions determine the fate of Amazonia.

What Is Amazonia?

Amazonia is the name given to the tropical forest of the Amazon River basin. It covers an area of approximately 2.3 million square miles

east of the Andes Mountain range in northern South America. The Amazonian wilderness covers an area about half the size of the United States. The elevation ranges from near sea level up to 5,000 feet, and the hot, muggy air exceeds 80 percent relative humidity for at least 130 days per year. The temperature is warm year round, with the average daytime temperature around 80 degrees Fahrenheit, although the oppressive humidity makes it feel much warmer.

The Amazon rain forest is found mostly in Brazil but also in parts of Bolivia, Peru,

Ecuador, Colombia, and Venezuela. The Amazon basin in Brazil makes up about one-third of all the tropical forests in the entire world.

Running through this huge region is the mighty Amazon River. The Amazon is not a single river but a vast, intricate network of waterways. There are at least 1,000 tributaries to this river, with 17 that are at least 1,000 miles long. The water carried by the Amazon is almost too great to measure. At its mouth, 7.5 million cubic feet of water flows by per second. Part of this water comes from the melting snow in the Andes Mountains, but most of it is from rainfall. Torrential rains fall on the forest, in excess of 80 inches per year. In the foothills of the Andes, rainfall may measure 150 inches annually. Author Nigel J. H. Smith describes the river in *The Enchanted Amazon Rain Forest:*

> The Amazon basin, with its myriad waterways extending from the rivers emptying into the pounding surf of the Atlantic shore in the east to icy Andean streams in the west, is home to more species of fish than any other watershed in the world. This aquatic wonderland, encompass[es] cool forest streams, thundering waterfalls, treacherous rapids, placid lakes, and sluggish channels.[1]

The Amazon rain forest straddles the equator and covers millions of acres of flat terrain. Pilots flying over the region can travel several hours without seeing a house, road, or field, the only landmarks are trees crowned with purple or yellow blooms that stand out above the dark green forest.

The forest contains an incredible range of life forms—it is rich with hundreds of plant and animal species found nowhere else on earth. Within a typical four-square-mile section of Brazilian rain forest there are 750 different species of trees. And in that same area there might be 125 different kinds of mammals, 400 types of birds, and 100 species of reptiles.

The Amazon's profusion of shrubs, trees, vines, ferns, and orchids contains hundreds of plants that are valuable as food and medicine, and for commercial uses. The harvesting of fruits, nuts, fibers, essential oils, and latex rubber provides income to millions of rural people who live along the forest's rivers, creeks, and roads.

The British naturalist Charles Darwin first viewed this awesome forest in the 1850s. Here is how he described the experience:

> Among the scenes which are deeply impressed on my mind, none exceed the sublimity of the primeval forests undefaced by the hand of man. No one can stand in these solitudes unmoved . . . the sensation of delight which the mind experiences. . . . The land is one great, wild, untidy, luxuriant hothouse, made by nature herself.[2]

Diverse plant and animal species thrive in the vast network of waterways and lush forest that make up the Amazon rain forest.

The Prehistoric People of the Amazon

Humans have lived in Amazonia for a relatively short time compared to how long they have been in Asia and Africa. The evidence shows that the first immigrants to the region might have arrived as recently as fifteen thousand years ago. (By comparison, humans have lived in Africa for hundreds of thousands of years.) The early settlers probably came overland on foot from Central or even North America. The settlers' lives in this region took place in deep isolation and without the influence of outsiders.

When the Amazon's people first came to the area, the weather was quite different from what it is like today. The climate of the lowlands was much drier, which made the forest growth smaller and less dense. As the centuries passed, however, the climate grew wetter and the forest filled in the open fields and grasslands. The area's forests provided hard woods for spear points, and vines, bamboos, and palms supplied material for baskets, nets, snares, and traps to catch game animals. The forests also held plants for food and medicine as well as poisons that were used for hunting.

The Amazon rain forest sits on some of the most ancient land formations on earth. The soil is so deep that stone is extremely difficult to find. The few stones there were to be found were valued by the natives to make axes. The leaves and wood that fall from the trees and plants decompose quickly and leave behind a thin layer of topsoil. Natives began farming this soil about three thousand years ago. They planted sweet potatoes and manioc (a shrubby plant grown for its large tuberous, starchy roots) in small fields that they cleared by burning.

Anthropologists often learn about ancient cultures by the rock and stone tools that they leave behind. But there is very little stone in the Amazon basin, so little is known about how its people lived. The early Amazonians made almost everything they owned from wood, bone, plant fibers, seeds, feathers, and other perishable materials. Such items are quickly destroyed in hot, humid climates like the Amazon basin's.

Natives Today

When the rain forest was first discovered by Europeans in the 1500s, about 6 million natives were living there. Today there are fewer

A Matses Indian harvests medicinal plants from the forest canopy. The Indians have used the forest's bounty for generations.

Contact with outsiders has altered life for indigenous tribes like the Waurá.

than 250,000. Only a small number of these people live in the primitive manner of their ancestors. These traditional peoples dwell in pole-and-thatch houses in small villages. Their principal cutting tool is the stone ax, and their main weapon is the bow and arrow. Their primary means of travel is the dugout canoe. They wear few, if any, clothes. The natives sustain themselves by hunting, fishing, agriculture, and gathering. They plant manioc, corn, cotton, tobacco, and various fruits.

The native populations in the Amazon can be roughly classified into five linguistic subgroups: the Ge-speaking people, the Tupis, the Panoans, the Caribs, and the Arawak. Although they share similar language bases, each tribe has developed in isolation, so each has its own specific language and culture. Anthropologists call the estimated 170 tribes that share these languages the lowland Indians. (Highland Indians are found in the mountainous regions of Peru, Colombia, and Ecuador.) The tribes with the largest populations are the Kayapó, the Mehinaku, the Waimiri-Atroari, and the Tukano. All of these tribes are threatened by the rapid advance of civilization into Amazonia.

The indigenous natives live in various ways in Amazonia. The people of the Yanomami tribe, however, make up the last truly primitive tribe left in the Amazon basin and the last such people anywhere on earth. They live in some 250 independent villages and number about ten thousand people. Most of the Yanomami live in Venezuela's southernmost state, Amazonas, which is a dense rain forest the size of Oklahoma. This area contains the headwaters of the mighty thirteen-hundred-mile-long Orinoco River, which empties into the Caribbean.

Incredibly, the Yanomami retained their native patterns of life until the early 1990s. Today most of their villages have had contact with outsiders. Powerful economic and cultural forces in Brazil and Venezuela are encouraging—or forcing—them to move closer to modern culture in the name of progress, development, or religion.

The Yanomami are called "the Fierce People" by outsiders. But, as author Donovan Webster writes in *National Geographic* magazine,

Despite their off-putting reputation, my visit with the Fierce People has been nothing but neighborly. When we arrived in [their village], for example, they greeted us with hoots and screams, their

The Threatened Natives of the Amazon **11**

The last truly primitive Amazon tribe, the Yanomami largely retained their traditional lifestyle until the early 1990s.

headman slapping us repeatedly on our chests and backs as a sign of welcome.[3]

Threats to the Forest

The Amazon basin remained a cultural and commercial backwater for centuries after its discovery by Europeans. There were a few boom-and-bust economic cycles, mostly involving the tapping of trees for rubber. But the years since 1970 have forever changed the face of Amazonia. Frontier roads have sliced across broad sections of the land. These highways brought tens of thousands of land-hungry poor people, who turned the magnificent forest into cattle pastures. Loggers with their buzzing chain saws began cutting the forest at an unprecedented rate—one logger with a chain saw can cut down a thirty-three-foot-wide, one thousand-year-old tree in just ten minutes. In addition, the discovery of gold brought miners whose excavations tore gaping holes in the earth.

The ecological impact of the development projects in the Amazon basin have ignited heated debate. The decimation of the world's largest forest has led to a disruption of rainfall, increased soil erosion, and more flooding in the region. It has also destroyed the forest's biodiversity.

The widespread scale of development and ecological change in Amazonia has stirred worldwide concern for the native peoples of the region. Few tribes have ever benefited from having contact with civilization. Some believe that the loss of their ancient cultural diversity is at least as serious as the loss of plant and animal species.

Every year more than 20 million acres of Brazilian rain forest is destroyed. This equals about 54,800 acres a day, or almost 2,300 acres an hour. At the present rate of destruction, the Amazon rain forest will disappear by the year 2050. But the native peoples, along with their ancient wisdom, will be gone long before then.

A Village Under One Roof

Even at the dawn of the twenty-first century, there are still some Indians in Amazonia who have not seen the face of a person of European descent. But the influences of Europe and North America have penetrated even the deepest forest. Machetes, knives, fishhooks, pots, pans, guns, and even boat motors have reached the most isolated tribes of Amazonia through a network of trade that joins some 350 villages. Tribes like the Yanomami are extremely skillful traders, always prepared to exchange valued objects from the outside world for other such items.

Besides trade, the lives of the primitive Yanomami revolve around gathering food and making the few material possessions they require. These items include baskets, hammocks, bows and arrows, and colorful pigments used to paint their bodies. Their lives are relatively easy, letting them survive by working only about three hours a day.

Yanomami women grow cotton in their gardens to make hammocks. They wrap a continuous strand of cotton yarn around the upright poles of the huts where they live. Then they plait cross seams every few inches to hold the strands in place. Comfortable cotton hammocks are in great demand, but many people make due with flimsier, less comfortable hammocks made from vines. Children sleep in the same hammocks as their mothers until they receive their own hammocks at age five.

Yanomami villages are round and open with a central common area. Everything is in

A Yanomami woman weaves a basket, a task that produces one of the tribe's few necessary material possessions.

public view. People can hear, see, and smell almost everything that is going on anywhere in the village. Privacy is rare. These villages may be as small as forty or fifty people or as large as three hundred. Until recently, when the detrimental effects of civilization reduced their numbers, Yanomami villages contained many more babies and children than adults. Life expectancy for the Yanomami is short—averaging only about thirty-five years.

Although the Amazon basin is marked by heavy rainfall, it does not rain all the time. The rainy winter lasts from May through November. The dry season—punctuated by cloudbursts and short periods of rain—lasts from December to April. This seasonal variation is important to the lives of the Amazon natives, who prefer the dry season over the wet. As Robert L. Caneiro writes in *People of the Tropical Rainforest*, "The Mekranotí of central Brazil . . . call the dry season *amex kam* 'good time,' while the wet season is just *na kam* 'rainy time.'"[4]

Water races into the rivers during the rainy season's downpours. Even small rivers may rise thirty feet or more in one night. Such flooding has forced some tribes, like the Shipibo in eastern Peru, to build houses with palm-wood floors raised several yards above the ground. This elevation allows floodwaters to pass harmlessly underneath.

During the unpredictable downpours of the rainy season, the Amazon's residents prefer to stay at home. In the dry season, however, the Indians spend their time trekking through the forest in search of food, visiting other villages, and organizing feasts and ceremonies.

Under the Roof of a *Shabono*

Deep in the Amazon forests of southern Venezuela, on the border of Brazil, the jungle foliage is emerald green as far as the eye can see. But here and there brownish rings of dried palm leaves poke through clearings.

Yanomami children play in the large, open plaza of a shabono, *the huge, donut-shaped huts that house a village of as many as one hundred people.*

These are the roofs of the twenty-five-foot-high *shabonos*, enormous donut-shaped huts where the Yanomami live. *Shabonos* are made of poles cut from the forest that are lashed together with vines and thatched with leaves.

More than twenty families may live together inside a typical *shabono*, with each family having its own hearth for cooking and for warmth at night. Inside a *shabono*, people sleep in hammocks strung up around hearth fires, which burn night and day. There are few personal possessions in a *shabono*. Wooden racks hold bananas and other food, and baskets, cooking utensils, and small numbers of tools hang from the walls. In the middle of a *shabono* is an open plaza where children play and adults hold celebrations. A *shabono* is an entire village under one roof.

Although a *shabono* is a communal house, each family builds its own section of the roof. The men do the heavy work, fetching poles, securing them in the ground, and weaving the thousands of leaves that go into the roof thatch. The women and children help with the thatching and gather leaves and vines.

The holes for a *shabono*'s main poles are dug with a machete, and the dirt is scooped out by hand. The thatching is woven between a series of long, slender saplings held in place by four large poles. After each family finishes its own section, separated by a few feet of open space, the thatch is woven between each area to give the village the appearance of one large circular roof with an open plaza in the middle. (Individual Yanomamis who are in close contact with outsider civilization tend to build single *shabonos* in the traditional manner.)

The Life Cycle of a *Shabono*

Building a *shabono* is one of the most labor intensive jobs undertaken by the Yanomami.

The effort requires a high degree of cooperation, planning, and many days of work. Once a *shabono* is finally finished, however, it is very pleasant inside—cozy and tidy, with the smell of fresh-cut leaves.

Shabono villages can accommodate eighty to one hundred people. A village that has a strong alliance with another one may have a guest area able to house up to one hundred visitors.

A *shabono* lasts about two years before its roof begins to leak. By that time the building has become infested with roaches, crickets, and other insects. Roaches become so abundant in the roofing material that they create a constant buzzing, which intensifies if someone brushes close enough to the roof to alarm the insects. Sometimes villages become so infested that roaches fall from the roof by the dozen and scurry away any time someone moves. These insects can be as big as birds or as small as ants. Old *shabonos* are burned to the ground so that their insect pests are exterminated.

Once a *shabono* is burned, a new one might be built in the same spot or nearby. A new site must be far enough away from the tribe's enemies but near land suitable for gardening, and it must be on a slight rise so as not to flood during the rainy season.

The weather affects a *shabono*'s construction. In some areas where the Yanomami live the elevation is twenty-five hundred to three thousand feet above sea level. Nightly temperatures may drop to sixty degrees Fahrenheit, and high humidity can make it feel like only forty degrees. In these places, a *shabono* might have large masses of banana leaves hanging from the ceiling to the ground to keep the warmth from the hearths within the sleeping area. Unfortunately, this also keeps the smoke in. But people who own neither clothes nor blankets can tolerate smoke if it means staying warm.

The Yanomami sleep on hammocks and are kept warm by hearth fires which burn night and day in the shabonos. *Sparse furnishings include food, cooking supplies, and few personal possessions.*

Wind is also destructive to *shabonos*. It blows the leaves away and can even rip off a roof completely. Sometimes the Yanomami throw heavy logs on roofs to keep them in place during windstorms. Renowned anthropologist Napoleon A. Chagnon describes another method of dealing with the wind in his book *Yanomamö: The Last Days of Eden:*

> The most common defense against wind is magical. The shamans rush forth and chant incantations at *Wadoriwä*, the spirit of the wind, pleading with him to stop the blowing. He seldom does. Often, the shaman of an enemy village is accused of causing the spirits to make the violent winds, and the local shaman retaliates by urging *Wadoriwä* to blow their roofs off, too.[5]

A *shabono* might be surrounded by a ten-foot-high palisade, or pole fence, if the villagers are afraid of enemy attacks. Such a palisade is kept in good repair if the threat of attack is high. If not, the fence's wood is periodically pilfered to supply the community's cooking fires. Village entrances are covered with dry brush at night to warn of an enemy attack. The loud rustling of someone walking through the brush alerts the village dogs, whose barking then wakes the villagers.

Traveling Through the Forest

The Yanomami are called foot people because, unlike many others in the Amazon, they do not use canoes but travel on foot. In times past, the Yanomami avoided the larger rivers and preferred to live on the plains between the rivers. To them, the rivers were obstacles that could be crossed only when they shrank during the dry season. Because they have stayed away from the larger rivers, the Yanomami's contact with outsiders, who travel by river, has been limited. However, the Ye'kwana, the Yanomami's neighbors to the north, are river people who travel extensively along the major waterways in long dugout canoes.

The dense canopy of the forest keeps sunlight from reaching the ground. On overcast days the jungle is dark and gloomy. From the inside it appears to be swathed in shades of gray, not green. Scrub brush and vines grow everywhere, making travel by foot difficult. Along rivers and streams, where sunlight can penetrate, luxuriant vegetation grows. These areas are havens for dozens of bird and animal species.

Yanomami villages are thinly scattered across the vast jungle landscape. Distance between the villages can be only a few hours' walk or as much as a ten-day trek. The warfare between certain villages serves to keep them widely separated. The villages are closer together when there are intervillage alliances between ancestors and friends.

The villages all have trails leading into the jungle, to other villages, or to nearby gardens. The Yanomami tend to make their trails directly through the brush, swamps, and hills rather than skirting around them. They constantly snap off twigs as they walk to mark their trails. Some of these trails are difficult to see, and only an experienced native can follow a seldom-used trail. The trails between friendly villages are well worn, however, and the most frequently used trails have temporary camping places along the way, including small lean-tos where travelers may spend the night.

When friendly neighbors visit, small groups of men carrying only bows and arrows can quickly travel the distances between villages. Women carrying babies and trade items might take twice as long to travel the same distance. When a whole village decides to travel to another one for a feast, the trek might take two or three days instead of the usual time.

Walking contains a certain risk for the Yanomami. They wear no shoes or clothing, so thorns pose a constant danger. A party can rarely walk for more than an hour before someone must sit down and dig a thorn out of a foot using an arrow point. While the Yanomami's feet are normally hard and callused, walking in streams and on muddy paths softens the calluses.

Travel and communications between villages stop during the rainy season. Long

The Threat of Snakes

When a group of Yanomami walk through the jungle, they consider it an honor to lead the party. But being the leader is also more dangerous because of poisonous snakes, which tend to bite the first person who disturbs them. A large number of the Yanomami die from snake bites, and almost all of them are eventually bitten. Most bites are not fatal, but they are painful. A few snakebites may be severe enough to cause the loss of a limb or limit its use. Anthropologist Napoleon A. Chagnon once wrote of a Yanomami man who had a leg that rotted away and fell off as a result of a snakebite. The man got around by hopping on one foot.

Snakebites occur as commonly near villages as they do on remote trails since snakes often frequent firewood piles and gardens. The Yanomami try to keep their gardens and paths free of weeds to deter rodents, which attract snakes.

stretches of trails are then under water, and basins turn into small lakes. If villagers must travel, they can make simple pole-and-vine bridges to traverse small streams. These bridges usually wash away within weeks.

The Daily Lives of Yanomami Men

Small Yanomami villages are overseen by a man called the headman. He is usually the smartest or most charismatic member of the tribe. The headman keeps order in his own village and determines its relationship with other villages. Headmen act either as peacemakers or valiant warriors, depending on the situation. Peacemaking usually involves the threat of force, and most headmen have reputations for being fierce.

Headmen generally get their positions from marriage or it is passed down to them from relatives. Headmen can sometimes use their wit, wisdom, and charm and rule like kings, but most of them are looked upon as equals by the rest of the tribe. They, too, must help clear the gardens, collect food, hunt, and plant crops.

None of the Yanomami wear clothing. A well-dressed Yanomami man wears nothing but a string of garden-grown cotton around his waist that is tied to the stretched-out foreskin of his penis. As a boy matures, he starts to act older by tying his penis to this waist string.

Traveling by foot and without protective clothing, the Yanomami are constantly plagued by thorns and snakebites on trails forged through brush, swamps, and hills.

Yanomami culture dictates that men wear nothing more than a cotton string around the waist. Many Yanomami men who have had contact with outsiders have switched to shorts and loincloths.

Sometimes an older boy or man will find that this arrangement has accidentally come untied—to his great embarrassment. To him, this is like being completely naked.

This string is so important that even in the heat of battle two men will stop fighting if one of the contestants comes untied. These penis strings are clearly uncomfortable, and when clothing is available at trading posts, men quickly become accustomed to wearing shorts or loincloths, at which point the practice of penis tying is discontinued.

The Yanomami are shocked if they meet outsiders who have been circumcised (had their foreskins removed at birth). In Yanomami culture the removal of a foreskin is reserved for those who have committed the dire crime of incest.

Warfare and Hostility

The Yanomami are fiercely independent. Political intrigue and warfare often exist between villages. Individual members of different villages may become allies, but they may still harbor distrust toward one another. During the dry season, when travel is easy, raiders may travel to distant villages and strike suddenly at unsuspecting enemies. Before the advent of civilization, the Yanomami fought with the club, bow, arrow, and spear. Sometimes arrows were tipped with poison. Today, however, the Yanomami employ guns and even axes and hatchets as weapons of war.

Physical aggression has played a large role in shaping Yanomami culture. Some villages have been raided hundreds of times over the course of the years, and the Yanomami tribespeople live in a chronic state of warfare that is reflected in their mythology, ceremonies, political behavior, and marriage practices.

Over the years, at least 25 percent of the males have died violently. Some warriors have killed as many as twenty people. Although such warfare still continues in isolated places, it has greatly diminished where civilization has approached Yanomami villages. In recent years

Considered inferior in their male-dominated society, Yanomami women are assigned the least desirable chores. One such chore is the collection of firewood, a difficult and time-consuming task.

the Yanomami have banded together to cooperate in saving their threatened way of life.

The Daily Lives of Yanomami Women

Yanomami society is based on the will and desires of the tribe's men. Anthropologists studying the culture hear statements such as "men are more valuable than women," or "boys are more valuable than girls."[6] Both men and women hope that their babies will be boys.

Female children are assigned chores around the tribe's *shabono* long before their brothers are. At an early age, girls are expected to tend to their younger siblings and to help their mothers in hauling water, cooking, and collecting firewood. By the time girls reach puberty they have probably been promised to some older man for marriage.

Women do not participate in the political affairs of the Yanomami and are assigned the most unpleasant chores. Collecting firewood, for instance, is a labor-intensive task. Women spend several hours each day scouring the nearby area for suitable firewood. There will be a good supply of firewood where trees have been chopped down or burned to make room for gardens. But after a year in the same location, that land will also be cleared. Then the women must forage farther and farther from the village, often traveling several miles in each direction.

Women can be seen leaving the village at about four o'clock in the afternoon. They will return at dusk, marching in a long line and carrying huge baskets of firewood. If a woman finds a good supply of wood near the village, she will hide it from the others. If she is lucky, she will have an ax to lighten her work.

Yanomami women bear many children and nurse them for up to three years. All women, except the very old, live in constant fear of being kidnapped by raiders. Accordingly, whenever they leave the village, they take their youngest children with them so that if they are abducted, they will not be separated from their children. This fear gives women a special concern when it comes to intervillage politics. Sometimes women will goad their men into fighting an enemy in hopes that the threat to their security will be reduced.

As a Yanomami woman ages she gains respect, especially if she has adult children. The oldest women occupy a unique position. They can travel from one village to another in complete safety—no one will harm them. As a result, they are often used as messengers between villages.

Marriage

The main social activity within native Amazonian villages is the giving and receiving of young girls for marriage. Marriages are generally arranged among the older male kin, usually through fathers, uncles, or brothers. This process is essentially a political one in which girls are promised in marriage at an early age by men attempting to create alliances with other men.

The general shortage of women that exists among the tribes is due in part to the fact that some men have several wives. Many battles arise over sexual conflicts or the failure to deliver a promised woman. Sometimes a married woman will simply be taken by another man. The fighting that results can lead to a village splitting up and the new groups becoming ferocious enemies.

Most such violence is controlled, however. It can be anything from chest pounding to duels with clubs or shooting guns into the air. This gives men a wide range of responses without having to resort to deadly violence.

Marriage also allows tribes to forge alliances with one another by exchanging of marriageable women between villages. But, as anthropologist Napoleon A. Chagnon writes,

no good thing lasts forever, and most alliances eventually crumble. Old friends become hostile and occasionally treacherous. The people of each village must remain keenly aware that their neighbors are fickle, and they must behave accordingly. The village leaders must traverse a thin line between friendship and animosity, employing political acumen and strategies that are both admirable and complex.[7]

Yanomami Fashion

Yanomami women use cotton to make decorative waistbands, armbands, and halterlike garments that they wear crossed between their breasts. Men, women, and children wear strands of cotton string around their wrists, ankles, knees, and chests. The women also wear short pieces of a plant called arrow cane in their pierced earlobes. Although women wear no other clothing apart from these garments, they do maintain a certain modesty about their nudity.

Both Yanomami women and men often wear the same hairstyles. They use a type of reed called *sunama* to trim their bangs and to shave their heads. This sliver of reed is wrapped around a finger and scraped over the scalp, neatly cutting the hair as efficiently as a razor blade. Men who have been clubbed over the head in battle like to show off their often grotesque scars by shaving a bald circle, called a tonsure, in the crown of their heads. The men highlight their scars by rubbing red pigment into them.

If head lice become bothersome, the Yanomami groom one another, picking out the insects, and eating or biting them to kill them. When this process becomes too time consuming—as it often is with children—they simply shave off the hair.

Yanomami girls have almost no voice in whom they will marry. They are used as trading pawns for their kinsmen, and their own wishes are given no consideration. A girl is typically promised to someone before she reaches puberty and often to someone considerably older. Sometimes the future husband even takes over raising her for the rest of her childhood, but she will not begin living with him as his wife until after her first menstrual period. Marriage does not change a girl's life very much, and there are no formal wedding ceremonies.

A Yanomami woman is expected to respond promptly to the wishes of her husband and to anticipate his needs. Wives who are slow to prepare meals or do other chores may be scolded or even beaten. The most serious punishments, such as physical abuse, are usually reserved for wives who have been sexually unfaithful. As in many other societies, spousal brutality exists among the Yanomami.

A woman who is treated badly by her husband has the option of fleeing her *shabono* to find a husband in another village, but this can be dangerous. If the new village proves to be weaker, the old husband may pursue her there and mete out severe punishment to her for having run away. He might even go so far as to kill his wife. Most of the women who flee their husbands do so to escape particularly violent and cruel men, and they usually seek out a stronger village. Fortunately, in most cases the women can count on their brothers for protection against an abusive husband.

The Lives of Children and Adolescents

The difference in status between male and female children is developed early among the Yanomami. Young boys are encouraged to be fierce and are not punished for hitting young girls or even their parents. Boys as young as four years old learn that hitting their parents with fists or sticks is an acceptable means of showing anger.

Yanomami boys learn to hunt with bows and arrows at an early age and are encouraged to be fierce and aggressive.

Children explore the world around them constantly. Thus, they become naturalists at an early age. Most twelve-year-old boys can identify twenty species of bees, note their appearance and behavior, and tell which ones make the best honey.

Young boys hunt lizards for sport with miniature bows and arrows. In another game, called "get the bee," boys and girls catch live bees and tie light threads to their bodies. The tied bees then fly away slowly, dragging the string straight out behind them. The children chase the bees and knock them down by throwing sticks or rocks. Sometimes older men lead the children on a mock raid. The children make a human dummy from leaves and shoot it full of arrows at the adult's command.

Girls are allowed to play, but their childhoods end sooner than the boys'. Girls are only an asset to their mothers when they are working. Boys, in contrast, spend hours playing together and have little responsibility until they are about twenty years old, an age when the girls will be married and already have several children. The young unmarried boys will spend their days trying to seduce women, most of whom are already married. Not surprisingly, this practice leads to much jealousy and fighting.

When a girl has her first menstrual period, she is confined to her area of the *shabono* behind a screen of leaves. Her old cotton garments are thrown away and replaced by new ones made by her mother or older female friends. During this week the girl is given little food. What food she does receive must be eaten with a stick, and she is not allowed to touch it in any other fashion. She speaks in whispers, and then only to her closest relatives. After this period of confinement, the young girl goes to live with her promised husband, beginning her life as a married woman.

Daily Life in a *Shabono*

A typical morning in a *shabono* begins with children crying and people talking softly even before the sun rises. Often the morning chill wakes people at dawn, causing them to stoke the hearths and go back to sleep. Men who have made plans to hunt will leave the village at this time. Since certain game birds sing before dawn, they are easier for hunters to find before sunrise.

By the time the sun is up, people are preparing breakfast: usually green plantains peeled and toasted over coals. Leftover meat is taken from its storage space—dangling over the hearth on a vine—and the best portions are given to the men.

To take advantage of cool morning temperatures, work begins immediately after breakfast. Men might go to the gardens and begin clearing brush, felling trees, planting cuttings, and doing all the other work of gardening. They will work until about ten o'clock, when it becomes too hot and humid to continue. Then they bathe in a stream and return to their hammocks for snacking and napping.

By midafternoon the *shabono* is once again almost empty. People are off collecting firewood, hunting, or doing other work. The men might return to their gardens around four o'clock and work until dusk.

The evening meal is the biggest of the day. This food is often the result of the day's hunt—usually meat in the form of small game birds, monkeys, fish, and other protein. Men and women alike help prepare the evening meals, but the women do more of the work. Dinner is usually eaten with the fingers while in one's hammock.

By the time dinner ends, it is almost dark. The fires are then stoked and dried brush is secured across the entrances to the *shabono*. Before lying down in their hammocks for the

Men and women share the job of preparing meals. A Yanomami man plucks a wild turkey in preparation for the evening meal.

night, people wipe the dirt and grime off the bottoms of their feet. Everyone sleeps as close to the fire as possible.

The village is usually quiet by the time darkness falls. But it may not stay quiet. Sometimes a prominent man will give long, loud speeches into the night, voicing his opinions about the world. Shamans might chant all night to rid someone of sickness. Likewise, someone mourning the dead could weep and wail all night long. Occasionally a domestic quarrel will explode and before long the whole village will join in screaming, cursing, and taking sides in the dispute between husband and wife. The shouting may continue for hours, die down, and then start again.

Name Taboos

The Yanomami have strict taboos against even mentioning the names of prominent people, living or dead. Thus, when a person dies, his or her name can no longer be used. To keep the loss of a person's name from making the language too inconvenient, the Yanomami use highly specific names, such as "whisker of the howler monkey" or "toenail of the sloth."

This name taboo applies even to the living. The mark of one's prestige in the tribe is the courtesy others show by *not* using one's name publicly. This custom is particularly true with men, who compete much more for status than do women. In one case a woman was married to a Yanomami headman for many years before she discovered his name.

As young boys grow up they demand that their names not be used and that they be called instead by kinship terms such as "brother of Himotoma." The better they are at having others avoid their names, the greater their social standing. The reasoning behind this name taboo involves a combination of fear, respect, admiration, political deference, and honor.

Outsiders living among the Yanomami usually have great difficulty dealing with this identification system. In a village where almost everyone is somehow related, it is difficult to designate the right person simply by saying, "Call your cousin for me." Anthropologist Chagnon learned this when he went to a Yanomami village to trace the natives' genealogies:

> The villagers quickly grasped what I was up to, that I was determined to learn everyone's true name. This amounted to an invasion of their system of prestige and etiquette, if not a flagrant violation of it, and their reaction was brilliant but devastating. They invented false names for everybody in the village, systematically learned them, and freely revealed them to me. I smugly thought I had cracked the system and enthusiastically spent some five months constructing elaborate genealogies.
>
> Since they enjoyed watching me work on the names and kinship relationships, I naively assumed that I was getting the most truthful information by working in public. This set the stage for converting my serious project into a hilarious game of the grandest proportions. Each informant would try to outdo his peers by inventing a name more preposterous or ridiculous than one I had been given earlier, the explanation for discrepancies being "Well, he has two names, and this is the other one." They even fabricated devilishly improbable genealogical relationships, such as someone being married to his grandmother or, worse yet, his mother-in-law—a grotesque and horrifying prospect to the Yanomami.[8]

As it turned out, the Yanomami were giving Chagnon obscene words instead of their names as a joke, and five months' worth of his research had to be thrown away.

Children and Spirits

The Yanomami believe that children are more likely than adults to be harassed by supernatural demons. A great amount of the tribe's sorcery deals with harmful magic that is believed to have befallen the young. Shamans constantly direct curses at the young people of enemy villages, and they spend just as much time warding off curses sent by other shamans.

Children are believed to be vulnerable to such attacks because their young souls are not yet established in their bodies. Their souls can wander out of their bodies at any time, most notably through the mouth when a child cries. Mothers, therefore, quickly hush their crying babies so that their souls cannot escape. The Yanomami believe that a child's soul can be recovered if the ground where it was lost is swept with a certain kind of branch.

Living on the Forest's Bounty

The daily lives of the Yanomami revolve around gardening, hunting, collecting wild foods, gathering firewood, carrying water, and making the few possessions they need for survival. The jungle provides the Yanomami with hundreds of types of plant and animal food. Some of these food sources are seasonal, others are available year round. Small groups of Yanomami may subsist entirely on wild food and game, but the majority depend on their gardens for food.

Food of the Forest People

Although wild food abounds, most Yanomami are farmers who grow produce in community gardens. They cultivate manioc (cassava), sugarcane, sweet potatoes, papaya, maize (corn), yams, and several varieties of peppers. Plantains—a kind of banana—are the main food source. They can be eaten green, roasted on coals, or boiled in pots.

Flatbreads made from manioc are another staple. To make them, women and children peel the tuberous roots of the manioc. They are then grated and the juices are pressed out through a basket. This paste is formed into thick flat cakes that are dried in the sun before they are baked.

Peach palm fruit, or *pupunha*, are important to Yanomami feasts. The nutritious fruit, which tastes like a chestnut, grows more than one hundred feet off the ground. Peach palm bark is covered with razor-sharp spikes.

Sometimes the Yanomami use a special ladder to reach the fruit at other times they stand on nearby trees and bring down the coveted peach palm fruit with vine lassos. On

A Yanomami boy bakes a flatbread made from manioc, one of many crops grown by the people of the Amazon.

the way back to the village, each adult might carry seventy to eighty pounds of fruit lashed on his or her back.

Wild honey is one of the Yanomami's most prized foods, and they will go to great extremes to harvest it. If someone spots a bee's nest, other plans for the day come to a halt and getting the honey becomes a top priority. Most kinds of honey are harvested by smoking out the bees and ripping the combs from the nest. The Yanomami eat the entire honeycomb, including the insect larvae it contains.

The Yanomami also live on a variety of other vegetable foods, including Brazil nuts, mushrooms, the seed pods of native bananas, and palm hearts.

Hunting

Of course, the forest consists of more than just trees. It is, in effect, a natural supermarket. But the forest does not easily give up its bounty, and Yanomami life is dominated by the search for food.

The Yanomami smoke straight-stemmed pipes filled with tobacco or herbs while they hunt. As they trek through the forest, the hunters sing together in beautiful lilting melodies or they sometimes screech and yell in high-pitched voices.

Since stone for spear points and arrowheads is quite rare, the Yanomami make projectiles from sharpened monkey bones, stingray spines, hard palm wood, and bamboo. Peach palm makes the strongest wood for bows, and the longest, straightest shafts for arrows come from a type of giant grass.

A six-foot-long arrow might be made by using a straight piece of cane for the shaft, a plug of hardwood for the butt, cotton fibers to hold it all together, and feathers taken from the *paruri*, a bird similar to a wild turkey, to make it fly straight. The arrowhead is then coated with poisonous resin from the bark of the virola tree, in the nutmeg family. When the arrowhead is shot into an animal, this poison will paralyze it within minutes.

The Yanomami make arrows of different sizes to kill larger or smaller animals. Their arrowheads are often painted red, black, or purple. Some arrows acquire a reputation or record for the game they have killed, and the arrow's history will be recited as it is traded to another owner. Buyers will raise their eyebrows, click their tongues, and express amazement at the trading partner's generosity at giving up such a fine piece of property.

Meat comes from a wide variety of animals, including giant anteaters, tapirs, armadillos, monkeys, wild pigs, wild boars, alligators, panthers, rodents, and wild game birds. The most commonly hunted game animals are two varieties of large birds that resemble pheasants and turkeys.

Once an animal is killed, its meat is preserved by smoking it at a base camp. After the hunters return to the village, the meat is boiled for several hours. The Yanomami have strong taboos about the appearance of blood in their food, so all of their meat is cooked thoroughly to make sure no blood will be visible while eating it.

When a dead animal is brought back to the village, the hunter will dance and stamp the earth to drive away the spirit of the beast so it will not remain in the village and cause trouble. Yanomami hunters believe that the spirit of the quick and agile hawk guides them in their hunting. They fear that the hawk spirit will abandon anyone who eats what he himself has killed. For this reason, Yanomami hunters share their kills with the others, confident that another hunter will be equally generous toward them.

Fishing

The Amazon and its tributaries teem with an astounding two thousand species of fish—eight times more than are found in the Mississippi River. At certain times of the year fish are plentiful and easily caught. At the end of the rainy season, for instance, many areas of the jungle begin to dry out as the rivers recede. The pools of water left behind are often stocked with dozens of stranded fish that can be easily caught by hand. Other fishing methods are necessary in the dry season when the rivers are low. Although fish are found in large abundance, the Yanomami diet relies more on game taken from the jungle.

Fishing is usually performed by women and children, but men often help. To catch fish, women hold large mesh baskets in the river's current and simply scoop them up from the water. Children help steer the fish into the baskets. Because electric eels infest the waters, the men stand upstream, spearing the eels to protect the women and children fishing.

Another fishing method involves the poisonous *ayori-toto* vine. Children help the men beat the vines with sticks so that the vines separate into fibers and its poisonous sap flows freely. Then the men sweep these vines through the rivers so that the poison stuns the fish, which rise to the surface. The women quickly scoop them up in baskets before the poison wears off. The *ayori-toto* poison breaks down quickly in the water, so it does not pollute the river. The fish that are not caught recover quickly and swim away.

Cooking and Eating

While Yanomami dinners are usually consumed while reclining in a hammock, some meals require family members to serve themselves by squatting around a common dish. Anthropologist Napoleon A. Chagnon describes one such meal:

> A large quantity of small fish is cooked by wrapping the fish in leaves and roasting them in the hot coals. Then the steaming package is spread open and everyone squats around it and shares the contents, alternating with bites of roasted or boiled plantain, and with a great display of finger licking, spitting out of bones, tossing away of inedible portions, and satisfied sighs.[9]

Animals are never skinned before they are cooked. They are simply put over the fire after their entrails have been removed. Then they are roasted—head, fur, claws, tail, and all. Most of the fur is burned off during the cooking process. Animals are usually cooked whole, but larger ones may be cut up before roasting or smoking them.

Planting and Harvesting

The manioc is the main subsistence crop of Amazonia. This shrubby plant is grown for its tuberous, starchy roots. The roots must be washed and dried carefully to remove all traces of the cyanide poison that occurs naturally in the manioc. (Manioc starch is also the source of tapioca.)

Maniocs are planted from cuttings, which are inserted one by one into the ground in mounds hoed up between charred stumps. Maize (corn) is planted from seeds dropped into holes that have been poked into the earth with digging sticks. Some of the other native crops that are grown include sweet potatoes, taro, yams, beans, and peppers. After contact with the Europeans began in the early 1500s, the Indians also started farming bananas, plantains, and peanuts.

The forest soil in Amazonia is soft and brittle and easy to till. But tangles of roots from trees prevent easy cultivation. Some tribes, like the Kuikuru, dig out the masses of rootlets and place them on the manioc cuttings to shield them from the sun. In some areas animals pose a serious threat to crops. Deer eat manioc leaves, and peccaries (a type of wild pig) eat the roots. Farmers are thus forced to build strong fences around their gardens to keep out the wild animals.

The warm Amazonian temperatures and abundance of rain create ideal growing conditions. Maize, the fastest-growing crop, can be harvested in less than two months. Manioc tubers take at least six to eight months to mature, but they will continue to grow underground without rotting for eighteen months or more.

When manioc tubers are finally pulled up from the ground, the stems of the plants from which the maniocs grew are cut into one-foot sections. These cuttings may be replanted immediately or, since these stems will last for months if protected from the sun, they may be set aside for replanting at a later date. A manioc garden is usually replanted two or three times before its yield is so seriously decreased that it is abandoned. A garden's eventual diminished yield is the result of lower and lower soil fertility and the choking effect of weeds that cannot be controlled in the jungle climate.

Chemical analyses have shown that most Amazonian soils are poor in the nutrients that plants need for growth. When a garden plot is cut and burned before planting, its soil is temporarily improved by the ash and decaying slash. But during cultivation, the crops draw on the nutrients added when the farmers burned the remaining stumps and

Making Bows, Arrows, and Poison

The wood used to make Yanomami bows is from a type of palm wood that is so dense and hard that a nail cannot be driven into it. The bow is painstakingly shaped by shaving it with the razor-sharp teeth removed from a wild pig's lower jaw. These bows are oval and very powerful, but they become brittle with time and eventually shatter. Bowstrings are made from fibers found on the inner bark of a tree. This bark is stripped off and twisted into long, thick cords by rolling the fibers between the thigh muscle and the palm of the hand. The resulting cord is so strong that it can also be used to hold up hammocks.

One style of arrow point is made from a type of palm wood. First, a foot-long splinter is weakened every two inches by notching it. Then a poison is put into the cuts so that when the arrow is shot into a monkey, the splinter breaks off inside the target and sends the poison into its bloodstream. The monkey then falls to the ground instead of dying high in a tree where it would be hard to reach.

The poison for the arrow comes from the *mamukure* plant, which is leached in hot water with vegetable ingredients to make the substance stick to the wood. Large leaves are wrapped around the poisoned arrowheads when traveling so that rain cannot dissolve the toxic substance. In some areas, natives use vegetable poisons that are also powerful hallucinogenic drugs. Sometimes a hunter will scrape the poison off an arrowhead and sniff it for the intoxicating effect it creates.

slash. The continual heavy rains and scorching sun also act to remove nutrients from the soil.

After a plot is abandoned, it will rapidly be taken over by weeds. Then after five years or so, small trees will spring up, shading the weeds and preventing further growth. After another twenty years, the larger forest trees will return. Occasionally plots of farmland are planted with fruit trees, which take about eight years to produce. They may mature and be tended by a farmer's descendants for decades. Peach palms, which produce a nutritious fruit, are also grown for their excellent wood, as mentioned earlier. Eventually, these plots, too, will be choked out by the thickening forest. At the end of the cycle, a grown-over plot may provide further food to natives when invading grasses serve to attract deer and other animals that can be hunted.

Building New Gardens After Moving

Sometimes, either because of the natural destruction of the *shabono* or because of warfare, the Yanomami are forced to move. Warfare may result from factions arising within a village, with one group being forced to leave while the other stays with the *shabono* and garden. To escape the wrath of their enemies, those driven from a village might walk for four or five days before establishing a new, distant location. In such a move the exiled group must start a new garden in the jungle.

Occasionally a group will begin a new garden in a distant area even before they have planned an attack. By planning for disaster, they are prepared to move quickly if necessary. And if the disaster never comes, the new garden may be used for a pleasant campground.

Making a new garden from scratch while feeding a group of up to one hundred people is not an easy task. This is especially true if a productive garden has to be abandoned without warning. Those who are fleeing have two choices: either move to a friendly neighboring village and live off of that garden initially, or live off of wild foods. Those living on wild foods will still visit friendly neighbors occasionally to enjoy their garden produce. Meanwhile, they will be busy clearing a new garden of their own and planting fast-growing crops that will feed them as soon as possible.

Some villages on the move may adopt a range of options. They may simultaneously begin a new garden, live off of the forest's bounty, sneak back to their old garden, live off of the food growing at the old site, or collect cuttings for the new site. But there are problems with this strategy, as described by Napoleon A. Chagnon:

> This pattern involves several risks. The first is the risk of being attacked at the old garden or getting into a fight there with members of the group who have stayed. The second risk is the new group's dependency on the allies who are providing food, refuge, or both. The Yanomami are quick to take advantage of those who are vulnerable, and the cost an ally is likely to extract is one of sexual license with the new group's wives, sisters, and daughters during their visits to the allied village. Disadvantaged groups expect this, and they can resist it only up to a point. . . . The best solution is to make the visits to the allies as short as possible, to extract the maximum amount of economic and political aid in that time, and then to repair either to another ally or to one of the gardens.[10]

Grubbing for Dinner

While the men hunt, the women and children search for termite nests, which resemble big brown globes plastered to the sides of trees. These nests each contain thousands of winged black termites and fat white grubs, or larvae, which are bigger and more nutritious than the adult termites. The women cut the nests in half with machetes, impale them on sticks, and tap the nests until the juicy grubs inside them fall onto leaf pouches placed beneath the nests. These grubs will then be taken back to the *shabono* and roasted on the family hearths.

Another favorite is the large, fat palm-pith grub. To find these insects, the Yanomami fell a large palm and eat its vegetable heart. Then they return about a week later and chop into the decaying tree to get at the soft, spongy pith inside. By then a species of insect will have laid its eggs in the pith and the eggs will have developed into large grubs, some the size of mice. The Yanomami can harvest about fifty or sixty such grubs from just one tree.

The Yanomami eat a squirming grub by biting it behind the head and holding it tightly in their teeth. A strong pull leaves the head and entrails dangling from the mouth. These are spit out and discarded. The rest of the grub is tossed, still squirming, into a leaf bundle. These bundles are later tossed onto a campfire and are roasted, leaving a fat, shriveled white grub that is eaten in one gulp. The fat is eagerly licked off the fingers.

While hunting for grubs, the Yanomami will also capture frogs, tadpoles, large snakes, land crabs, and caterpillars to eat. The women also use these expeditions to search for vines that can be woven into baskets.

Maize is the best food for jump-starting a new garden. Its seeds are light, easy to transport, and it grows rapidly in the tropical climate. But maize is a less desirable food than plantains or maniocs because it is less filing and not as versatile for cooking. Plantains are transplanted by cutting suckers from a larger plant. And these suckers are large, heavy, and difficult to transport over a long distance. One Yanomami man might be able to carry only six or eight of these suckers in his arms.

In general, having to move quickly is not the biggest threat facing the farmers of the forest. The Yanomami can obtain adequate food with only several hours' worth of work a day. As long as the forest is large and the population small, slash-and-burn farming is well suited for humans to live in harmony with the environment. The portion of the forest cleared and planted by a village is a tiny fraction of the whole. But pristine areas where Indians can practice this manner of farming are fast disappearing. The survival of traditional slash-and-burn farming is more and more threatened with extinction.

Slash-and-Burn Agriculture

The traditional Indian tribes in Amazonia survive by using a farming technique that is known as slash-and-burn swidden, or shifting, farming. Many variations of this technique are practiced throughout the wet tropics, but the method is similar in the region.

First a section of forest is cut down. Then this slash is allowed to dry and is burned

Addicted to Tobacco

The main nonfood crop grown by the Yanomami is tobacco. It is so important that the Yanomami word meaning to be poor, *hori*, means "to be without tobacco." Men, women, and children as young as ten are ad-

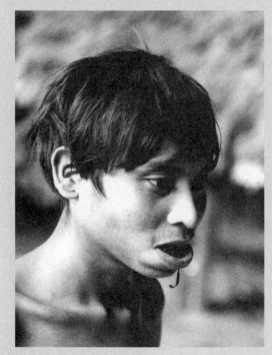

A young man chews tobacco, the crop most highly valued by the Yanomami.

dicted to this plant, which they chew and smoke. Each family tends its own tobacco patch and jealously guards it from theft—a common problem if a neighbor's supply runs out. Some Yanomami are so protective of their tobacco patches that they bury booby traps in them. These traps typically are sharp splinters of bone that can remain in a poacher's foot for a long time.

After the tobacco is harvested, its leaves are tied together and hung over a hearth to cure in the heat and smoke. The dried leaves are stored in large balls that are wrapped with another type of leaf to keep out insects and moisture. When it is to be used, leaves are peeled off the ball, soaked in water, and rolled in ash from the campfire. Finally, this ashy leaf is rolled into a short, fat cigarlike wad and bound with fine fibers to hold its shape. The user then lights up the wad and smokes it, usually while lying in his or her hammock.

If a user lays down his wad even for a minute, someone else may snatch it up and suck on it until the owner wants it back. The borrower might be a small child or his wife, a friend, or even a stranger. Scientists have traced this type of tobacco sharing to the spread of viruses and infectious diseases at both the village and the regional level.

---

before the start of the rainy season. A variety of crops are planted before—or after—the burn. The same plot may be planted two or three times from season to season, but with progressively smaller yields each time. The area will finally be abandoned and a new plot will eventually be cleared.

Before large trees can be brought down under this method, the thick forest undergrowth around them must first be cleared.

This is a difficult task even with machetes. Before these tools were introduced, however, the natives had to pull up the undergrowth by hand, break and bend small plants, or cut through the growth with a piranha jaw or a palm-wood knife.

Once the undergrowth has been thinned, the Indians turn their attention to the large trees. Before the arrival of Europeans, with their iron implements, a stone ax was the principal tool used to cut down trees. In forests with some of the hardest woods in the world, this was a major task involving many days of sweat, blisters, and aching muscles. First, the Indians would cut all the way around the trunk of the tree using a stone ax, so it looked like it had been felled by a beaver. German ethnologist Karl von den Steinen vividly describes this process:

> How tired a Bakairi (a native Indian) gets cutting down a single tree! Early in the morning when the sun rises he begins wielding his stone axe. The sun climbs the sky and the Bakairi continues to chop: tsok! tsok! tsok! His arms get wearier and wearier. The Bakairi rubs them and then lets them hang limply at his sides. He lets out a deep breath. . . . He resumes chopping, but no longer tsok! tsok! tsok! Now it is accompanied by deep groans. The sun reaches zenith. His stomach is now nothing but folds of skin—it is empty. How hungry the Bakairi is! . . . Finally, when the sun is right near the horizon, a tree falls![11]

To ease the work required, the largest trees were often girdled, which is a technique of removing a layer of bark from around a tree so that it cannot receive nutrients and eventually dies. Fire was also used to ease the process. In addition, when large trees were felled, they were directed at smaller ones that were notched slightly to make them fall against even smaller trees. This domino effect

A fire blazes out of control in the rain forest. Slash-and-burn farming, practiced by the peoples of the rain forest, requires the clearing and burning of land.

also served to remove tree crowns and the tough vines that grew between them. Although the natives now use metal axes, cutting down thirty-three-foot-thick, one-thousand-year-old trees by hand is still an arduous effort.

The felling of trees begins as soon as the rainy season ends. First, the slash is allowed to dry for several months. Then, when it is time to burn the area, the farmer walks through his plot with a torch, setting small fires every few feet. This connects into one huge fire, which burns quickly. After the fire burns out there are usually many stumps and trunks that are only charred. These remains are piled up and set afire once again.

Even with this reburning, many logs and stumps are left behind, giving a slash area a messy appearance. Charred logs are strewn everywhere, crisscrossing each other. During the three or four years that the plot will be cultivated, many of these logs will be cut up and hauled away for firewood or for fencing. The weeds pulled up from the new garden

A photograph clearly shows the damage caused by slash-and-burn agriculture, which destroys both the land and appearance of the rain forest. The method is ecologically sound when practiced on a small scale by the Yanomami, but harmful when used to clear large tracts of land for cattle pastures.

Manioc, the main subsistence crop of Amazonia, is harvested from the ground. Manioc gardens are replanted two or three times from stem cuttings.

are also piled up against stumps, then dried and burned. In this manner, after only a few years the area takes on the look of a permanent field with only food crops growing in it.

Trekking in the Dry Season

When the dry season arrives, an entire Yanomami village—except the sick and the old—may leave on a *waiyumö*, a trek lasting several weeks. During the *waiyumö*, the travelers live mainly on wild fruits, roots, and grubs, but they also bring along plantains in case food becomes scarce. When night falls, the men make crude hammocks out of bark stripped from trees. A triangular lean-to called a *yano*, is then built over the hammock, using poles and large leaves to keep off the rain.

Camping treks are a time of fun for the Yanomami. They afford a break from the work of gardening and provide a welcome change of diet. The dry season is also a time for visiting distant relatives and extending invitations for feasts, dances, and ceremonies with other villages.

3 Living in the Spirit World

The material world of the Yanomami and other Amazon natives is simple and uncomplicated. Their physical world contrasts sharply, however, with the richness and depth of their spiritual world. The Yanomami hold an elaborate, expressive set of beliefs about the cosmos, the soul, the mythical world, and the plants and animals around them.

Because they lack a written language, the Yanomami must store thousands of words in their heads—they cannot look up a word in a dictionary when they need one. Thus, the language has grown to be complex. Yanomami speakers delight in making poetic use of words in stories about the cosmos and their place in it.

The Four Layers of the Yanomami Cosmos

The Yanomami believe that the cosmos is made up of four parallel layers. Each section is curved, round, thin, and rigid, with a top and bottom surface. The edges of some surfaces are thought to be brittle and fragile. To walk on them would be like walking on a rotten roof where a person's feet break through in places. But many mythical events happen in this region, which is a netherland of dangerous spirits.

The top layer of the cosmos is thought to be pristine or tender. The layer is a void, but many things are thought to have originated there in the distant past. It is described as abandoned and nonproductive, like an old garden. This layer plays only a minor part in Yanomami life—it is just there.

The next level down is the sky layer. The top surface of this layer is invisible but is thought to be like the earth with gardens, trees, villages, animals, plants, and so on. Most importantly, the top edge of the sky layer is where the souls of dead Yanomami live. These souls are seen as being just like the living—they hunt, garden, make love, eat, and practice witchcraft on each other.

The underside of the sky layer is visible to the Yanomami. The stars and planets are attached to this layer and move across it, each on its own separate path. Some Yanomami think the stars are fish. They have no names for what we call the constellations. Modern Yanomami repeatedly ask outsiders whether they bump into this sky layer when they are in airplanes, which were rarely seen until the mid-1960s. (Today airplanes and helicopters are commonly observed over the Amazon.)

The Yanomami live on the third level down, which they call "this" layer. "This" layer has jungles, rivers, animals, hills, plants, gardens, and everything else contained in the world. The people other than the Yanomami who live on "this" layer speak a dialect that is "crooked," or wrong. They are called *nape*, meaning "less than human."

Foreigners are thought to dwell in *shabonos* just as the "real humans," the Yanomami, do. But outsiders are thought to be inferior copies of the Yanomami. Anthro-

The Yanomami view outsiders as subhuman and are puzzled by airplanes, which they think bump into the starts and planets that are visible in the sky.

pologist Napoleon A. Chagnon describes what the "real people" thought of him:

> The Yanomami thought I was a reincarnated version of a Yanomami, and they frequently asked if I had drowned and come back to life. The logic behind the question was that in one of their myths a great flood had occurred, and some Yanomami had escaped drowning by grabbing onto logs. They floated downstream, were not seen again, and presumably had perished. But some are returning, floating on logs (canoes), who

look different and speak "crooked"—foreigners. A spirit named Omawä fished them out of the water downstream, wrung them out, brought them back to life, and is returning them home.[12]

Although the Yanomami think of outsiders as being subhuman, they still wish to understand the ways of the *nape*. As one headman told *National Geographic* reporter Donovan Webster:

> The great flood came, and washed some of the people down the river, where they

learned new things. They became subhuman, nape. But some of what they learned I would like to know. Their medicine. The material from which they make hammocks (nylon). Their steel. But I would have to give up my life here. And why? To have what the nape have! [He stirs his fire with a stick. Sparks fly.] I am like all men, I want to know my future—then I want to control it. It is not possible.[13]

The final layer in the Yanomami universe is the surface below "this" layer, which is barren. A strange type of Yanomami are said to live here, a people called the Amahiri-teri. They originated long ago and fell from the sky layer, hit "this" layer, and continued to fall. Unfortunately for the Amahiri-teri, they fell only with their *shabonos* and gardens, not the jungle where they hunted. Thus, they have no game animals and have turned into cannibals. They are thought to send spirits up to "this" layer to capture the souls of children, then carry them down and eat them. To fight back, some shamans spend their days obstructing the Amahiri-teri, attempting to halt their cannibalistic journeys.

The Yanomami think that humans have a strong basic urge to become cannibals and could do so at any time. They believe they must constantly oppose this possibility. This strong fear of cannibalism crosses over into their eating customs, as Napoleon A. Chagnon describes:

Whenever I was hunting with them and we shot a tapir, I would cut off a thick juicy slice of tenderloin and fry myself a rare-cooked steak dripping with red delicious juice (blood). This so disgusted the Yanomami that they could not even watch me eat, and they would accuse me of wanting to become a cannibal or a jaguar,

which to them was a disgusting eater of raw human flesh. For their part, they overcooked their meat so badly that one can almost drive nails with it.[14]

Myths and Spirits

The Yanomami believe that the first, or original, humans were part spirit and part human. These people they call the *no badabö*, and they figure into dozens of myths about the origins of plants and animals. The *no badabös* are the spirits of living things. Some of these characters are quite funny and some of their actions are the cause of much laughter and hilarity. The Yanomami believe, for example, that Iwäriwä, the spirit of fire, was tricked into sharing fire with everyone during an obscene act that made him laugh, allowing the fire to escape from his mouth. Yanomami men love to take hallucinogenic drugs and prance around the village retelling this story with creative embellishments. They recount Iwäriwä's tone of voice, the gestures he made, and other details meant to amuse and entertain listeners.

The basic Yanomami creation myth says that men were created when an early form of humans shot the moon in the belly. The moon's blood fell to earth and changed into men. Where the blood was thickest, the men became fierce and killed each other. But where the blood fell only in droplets or mixed with water, the men were gentler and controlled their violence. These men, however, were lonely. One time when a headman picked a fruit called a *wubu* he noticed it had eyes. As the headman threw the fruit to the ground it changed immediately into a woman. She followed the headman back to his village, where all the men copulated with her. She had a baby daughter, then another and another, until finally there were enough women for the men.

When a Yanomami dies, his or her soul is said to escape up the ropes of his hammock and rise to meet the next layer of the cosmos. Then, it follows a trail until it comes to a fork, where the son of Thunder asks the soul if it comes from a generous person or someone stingy. If that person was stingy, the soul is directed down the fork on the path that leads to fire. If the person was generous, the soul is directed down the other path to *hedu*, where a tranquil, heavenlike existence awaits.

Unlike the heaven and hell beliefs of which outsiders often believe strongly, the Yanomami do not take this myth too seriously. When asked about it they say, "Well, [the son of Thunder] is kind of stupid. We'll just lie and tell him we were generous, and he'll send us to hedu."[15]

Another portion of the Yanomami soul is said to be released upon the body's cremation. It wanders around the earth and lives in the jungle. Some of the wandering spirits are evil and attack travelers in the jungle at night. They have bright, glowing eyes and beat the living with clubs and sticks. (The Yanomami who have come to civilization for the first time fear automobiles at night because they believe that the glowing headlights are the eyes of the evil spirits.)

Another portion of the Yanomami spirit is believed to live in or near the liver. This portion, which can be lured out and stolen, is vulnerable to supernatural attack. A person who loses this part of his soul will become ill and die. If someone becomes sick, shamans usually direct their healing powers at that person's liver.

A Yanomami man enters into a hypnotic trance after inhaling powder derived from the yakowana *tree. The Yanomami use various hallucinogenic drugs to help them come into contact with the spirit world.*

Shamans

The word shaman originated in Siberia, but it has been widely used to describe men and women of any tribal society who manipulate the spirit world, cure the sick using magic, diagnose illness, and prescribe magic remedies. In general, shamans intercede between the human world and the spirit one in matters of sickness and health.

Only Yanomami men can become shamans. Any man can do so, however, and in some villages a large number of the men are shamans. As in other religions, shamans, called *shabori*, must train for the position. For the Yanomami this begins with long periods of fasting, which can go on for a year or more. During this time the novice loses a great deal of weight and may be on the verge of death.

The older men instruct the novices in the songs, mysteries, and ways of the shaman. Novices try to attract tiny humanoid spirits, called *hekura*, to dwell within their chests. This requires much time and patience because the *hekura* are said to be fickle. During this period the novices also forsake sex, for the *hekura* are considered to dislike sex. The inside of a shaman's body is thought to be a heavenlike cosmos of rivers, streams, mountains, and forests where the *hekura* can dwell in happiness.

There are said to be thousands of *hekura*, ranging in size from a few millimeters to an inch or two. The *hekura* have glowing halos around their heads, are exceptionally beautiful, and are fond of hills or tall trees, where they may live. Most are named after animals. Some are physically hot to the touch while others are meat-eaters and are cannibalistic; the meat-hungry *hekura* are the ones shamans send to devour the souls of enemies.

Shamans call the *hekura* down from their trails in the sky or upon the mountains. The *hekura* come out of these areas reeling and dancing, glowing and fluttering in ecstasy like butterflies. The spirits enter a shaman's body at the feet and go to the liver, where their symbolic villages, forests, and mountains are to be found. Once they are in the body, they must follow the will of their human hosts, who send them out to devour their enemies or cure sickness in the village.

The Use of Hallucinogenic Drugs

Yanomami shamans believe that in order to contact the *hekura* in the spirit world they

A shaman from a Brazilian tribe treats an injured patient. Most tribal societies rely on magic and contact with the spirit world for the healing of illness.

A Young Man Becomes a Shaman

Young men often receive the calling to become shamans when they are about fifteen. At that time, they begin to practice chants, rhythms, and struts. Eventually, the older shamans begin to guide the young men. In the article "Amazon Grace," in the March 1997 issue of *Natural History*, author Kenneth Good describes the ordeal of an apprentice shaman named Rinawe:

"[Rinawe] must present himself as a worthy host to the spirits. Day after day he sits on the ground in the communal house, his legs extended in front of the headman's section, taking large doses of ebene and repeating the phrases chanted by the master shaman. As the spirits, summoned and encouraged by the master, approach Rinawe, the youth is overcome and falls prostrate on his back. A village mate props him up and holds him steady as the shaman blows more drugs into him and continues with his instruction.

After five days of taking ebene, and almost no food or water, Rinawe is emaciated and covered with dried mucus, ebene, and soil. He is so weak that he appears barely conscious, and his repetitions of the shaman's phrases are almost inaudible. Will the spirits come? Will they accept him? Or will they flee, depriving him of his hopes of becoming a shaman? Some women begin to cry in fear for Rinawe's life and from compassion for his ordeal. Even one of the men sitting close to the participants begins to sob."

Rinawe survives his ordeal, however, and after several years of training enters the venerable realm of the shaman.

must first consume hallucinogenic drugs. The jungle supplies several prized plants that the Yanomami use to make psychedelic snuff powder. The most common one is the soft, moist inner bark of the *yakowana* tree, which is dried and ground into powder. This is added to the snowy white ashes of another type of tree bark. The mixture is then moistened with saliva, kneaded into a gummy substance, dried on a fragment of broken pottery over a fire, and ground into a fine green powder.

An even more desirable hallucinogen comes from the *hisiomö* tree, whose tiny, lentil-sized seeds are peeled and packed into ten- or fifteen-inch-long wads to be used in trade. This tree is rare; the villages located next to a natural grove of it specialize in the *hisiomö* trade. This drug and others like it are known by the generic name of *ebene*. New batches of this drug are made every day, and it takes much kneading, pounding, and grinding to produce four ounces of the drug, which is enough for several men.

Only men take these drugs. Since the spirits the shamans hope to attract respond to beauty, they decorate their chests and stomachs with red pigment, don their best feathers, and do their best to make themselves attractive. The drugs are taken by placing them in long hollow tubes called *mokohiros*. One person blows the drug up another one's nose, once up each nostril. The recipient typically chokes, gasps, grimaces, and rubs his head with both hands. His eyes begin to water and his nose runs so profusely that long strands of green mucus drip from each nostril. Sometimes he falls to the ground, dizzy and stunned, convulsing with dry heaves and vomiting.

A *shaman (left) inhales hallucinogenic* yakowana *powder blown through a* mokohiro *tube as a means of contacting the tiny spirits that are believed to live inside a shaman's body.*

Anthropologist Chagnon writes about the *ebene*'s effects:

> Within a few minutes, he is having difficulty focusing and starts to see spots and blips of light. His knees get rubbery, and he walks as if he has had too many cocktails. Profuse sweating is also common, and the recipient's pupils get large. Soon the hekura spirits can be seen dancing out of the sky and down from the mountaintops, rhythmically prancing along their trails to enter the chest of their human beckoner, who by now is singing melodically to lure them into his body, where he can control them—send them off to harm his enemies or cure his sick kinsmen.[16]

When the shamans take *ebene* to contact the spirits, they begin singing soft, melodic, beautiful songs to attract the *hekura*. Then, as the *ebene* begins to take effect, the shamans start to sing progressively louder until finally they may be screaming. They recite the deeds of the *hekura* and sing creation songs. Since these performances take place almost every day, the other villagers tend to ignore them, but some may listen to the songs and remind the shaman that he left out a gesture or a story. In general, everyone knows these stories, which have been circulated for centuries.

Sometimes a young shaman will take too much *ebene* and will have a bad experience. Others may take *ebene* simply because they want to get high: They have no interest in the *hekura*. In some villages men take the drug every day, but in others its use is less common. Although the effects of the drug are evidently pleasant to those partaking of it, the ritual itself can seem unpleasant to observers.

Besides vomiting and discharging green mucus, the men engaged in the ritual may become violent and threaten to shoot someone or attack them with a machete. In some cases the violence becomes real. In one village a man chopped off the head of another with a machete while he was high on *ebene*. This resulted in the village splitting up and a protracted war between the once-united people.

The Art of the Feast Ritual

Although *ebene* plays a major part in daily Yanomami life, it has a less important role in the most joyous Yanomami ritual, the feast. Ritual feasts are held whenever one group wants to entertain members of an allied village. The main purpose of such a feast is to cultivate or maintain friendly relations between villages. Feasts help reduce warfare, expand marriage possibilities, and cement trade relations between groups.

The first feasts between groups take place only after one group of men has traded with another for as long as several years. Only then

A Shaman Heals a Nurse

Although Western medicine has now penetrated the Yanomami world, sometimes even the Western doctors go to a shaman to make themselves feel better. In his book *Amazon Journal*, Geoffrey O'Connor writes about Sister Florence, a nun at the Mission Catrimani in the Amazon rain forest. This tall, stocky black woman from Guyana speaks fluent Yanomaman and spends her days giving malaria shots and other medical care to the natives. During one of her typical twelve-hour work days, Sister Florence felt that she might be getting sick herself. At that point, O'Connor asked her what was wrong:

"'How are you feeling, Florence?'

'I'm not certain,' she responds. 'I think I might be [coming down with malaria.] . . . I have not tested my blood but I know too well the symptoms.'

At this point [an] older shaman . . . asks Florence a question in [Yanomaman]. . . . A minute later Florence calls me over.

'This man is going to do some shamanism,' she says.

'On who?' I say.

'On me. I told him I was sick and he offered to help me.'

'Do you believe in shamanism, Florence?'

'Yes.'

'Forgive me. But I don't understand. How can you believe—'

'—in shamanism?' she says. . . . I've seen what they can do. A shaman tells me a baby is sick and goin' to die then that baby dies. There is nothing I can do. He tells me a baby goin' to get well, the baby gets well." She flashes that crazy smile of hers.

'But you also take their cure?'

'They take my medicine and I take theirs.'

A few minutes later . . . the shaman begins his preparations for the curing ceremony. Florence, in her long blue nun's habit, sits beside her naked healer, quiet and patient.'"

do the nervous outsiders come to another group's village, many times leaving the women behind, hidden in the forest. Often the mutual suspicions eventually give way to confidence between groups, reciprocal feasting, and trading of marriage partners.

A feast is a joyous experience for the Yanomami. There are huge quantities of food, exciting dances, and open admiration of decorations and body painting. Eating is often taken to extremes, as described by Napoleon A. Chagnon:

> Some villages provide so much food that participants compete in drinking enormous quantities of banana soup or peach palm gruel, which they then vomit up and return for more. The plaza becomes dotted with large pools of vomit, and one must be careful where he walks—and careful not to walk in front of a celebrant who is about to regurgitate.[17]

Meat is not usually eaten during a feast, but hunters kill a large amount of game to be presented to the guests *after* the feast. The night before such a hunt, the young people of the village dance and sing in a ceremony designed to ensure the hunters luck. Only the finest meat is earmarked for the guests, and the hunters are not allowed to eat their bounty while they are out hunting. During that time they subsist on lesser game, such as small birds, insects, and fish.

Before feasts, huge quantities of plantains are cut and ripened for a week or so before being boiled into a sweet soup. On the day of the feast, up to one hundred gallons of plantain soup is served in three troughs made of tree bark. The soup preparation, usually done by the young men, takes all day. Meanwhile, the men are taking *ebene* and the women are putting the final touches on baskets they have made for the guests.

Traditionally, a feast begins only after the host village sends a messenger to the guests with a formal invitation. As the hosts prepare for their guests, the excitement builds. People paint themselves elaborately with red and black pigment and don colorful feathers.

The Ceremony

A feast starts as the guests gather outside the host village. They, too, are finely painted and come bearing gifts such as baskets and arrows. At a given signal, two dancers from the visiting group burst into the village and dance around the outside of the plaza. They are welcomed by shouts and shrill screams. The rest of the visiting dancers then follow, two at a time, dancing wildly to show off their decorations and weapons. Every dancer represents one family. Napoleon A. Chagnon witnessed one such feast:

> Each dancer had unique decorations or a unique dance step to exhibit. He might burst into the village, screaming a memorized phrase, wheel and spin, stop in his tracks, dance in place, throw his weapons down, pick them up, aim them at the line of hosts with a fierce expression on his face, prance ahead a few steps, and then repeat the whole performance as he continued around the clearing. The hosts . . . would cheer wildly.[18]

After the dancing, the hosts approach their guests. Each man invites one or more dancers into his house, leading the guest by the arm. The families of the dancers, who have been watching from the village entrance, join him at his host's house and jump into the host's hammocks. The guests are served the first round of soup, then treated to the sight of the hosts dancing around the clearing.

A ritualistic dance performed for guests is part of the feast ritual, an elaborate, joyous event that helps to maintain good relations between villages.

After a day of eating soup, night starts to fall. At this time, a marathon of chanting begins. One man chants softly and bids a visiting man to come join him. As the second man repeats the first one's phrases, the men turn to face each other. The host then recites a ritualistic monologue punctuated by staccato screams. The guest responds by twisting his body and answering with a rhymed, counterpointed, or scrambled version of the phrase.

Words and phrases are volleyed back and forth in this host's game of verbal Ping-Pong. When it is over, the guest then starts his own chant and invites a new man from the host village to join him. The process continues until dawn. During these chants the men often reveal to each other what they would like to receive during the next day's trading.

Early the next morning the hosts and visitors begin trading. A visitor will first ask the host headman for an item he wants. That item is then produced and dropped on the ground at the feet of the man who requested it, but he ignores it at first while his friends examine it in great detail, either praising it or listing its defects. In every trade, the hosts will argue that they have been too generous and the guests will complain that they have not been given enough.

The trading is fast, conducted with considerable arguing. Part of the ritual is for the hosts to hide their most cherished items and deny owning them. Guests also hide trade items. The trading is concluded by eight or ten o'-clock in the morning. At that point the visitors are given large baskets of food to take home: boiled plantains with smoked meats on top.

Two men from neighboring tribes engage in a chest-pounding duel in order to settle a dispute.

The Chest-Pounding Ritual

Occasionally a feast or trading session will go badly and fighting will break out. When this happens, a ritual of chest pounding begins. Two men will face off while the other men gather around, screaming, yelling, brandishing weapons, and urging on their companions. One man will typically spread his legs apart, puff out his chest, put his arms behind his back, and challenge the other man to hit him.

The opponent will size him up, adjust the victim's limbs or chest to give himself the best advantage, and make several dry runs. Then he will wind up like a baseball pitcher and deliver a crashing blow to the left side of the vic-

tim's chest with a closed fist. The victim's knees will often buckle as he staggers around, silently, shaking his head for several minutes. The crowd will cheer, click their tongues, and urge the victim to absorb another blow. The opponent is allowed to deliver as many as four punches in a row. If the victim finally falls to the ground, the opponent will dance around him while growling and screaming.

If the victim withstands the blows, he will be permitted to strike his opponent as many times as he was struck. If the opponent falters, the other side will cheer wildly. When one man finally drops out, a fresh opponent will challenge the victor. The reward for winning this duel is status; chest pounders earn a reputation of being fierce.

Cremation and Death Rituals

A long tradition of conflict exists between Yanomami village groups. The cause is often sickness or death. The Yanomami blame most deaths on harmful magic. They suffer a high infant mortality rate because of a wide variety of illnesses. To the Yanomami, babies die because someone has sent harmful spirits (*hekura*) to steal their souls. Or someone may have blown magic charms from far away that cause them to sicken and die.

Although cannibalism itself is repugnant to the Yanomami, they eat the ashes of their dead. When someone dies, his or her body is carried to a clearing in the village. The body is placed on a pile of firewood and wood is piled on the body. A fire is then ignited. Before that, however, children and those who are sick are sent away from the village because the Yanomami believe that smoke from a corpse can contaminate their souls. After a cremation, Yanomami men wash their bows and arrows to remove any contamination, and someone attends the fire to make sure the corpse is completely burned, especially the liver. If the liver does not burn fully, it is believed that the person committed incest during his or her lifetime.

When the ashes are cooled, they are carefully sifted and saved. First, any unburned bones and teeth are picked out and saved in a hollow log. Then, a close friend or relative of the deceased pulverizes the bones. This powder is carefully poured onto a leaf and is transferred to hollowed gourds. The dust and ash that remain in the hollow log are rinsed with boiled plantain soup. The resulting stew is drunk by the assembled friends and relatives of the dead, who mourn loudly, weeping

Abandoning the Shaman's Ways

Occasionally a Yanomami shaman will abandon his calling. In the March 1997 issue of *Natural History*, a village leader named Shoefoot describes his conversion to Christianity.

"As the years went on, the responsibilities of a shaman weighed heavier and heavier upon me. I was tired. So many sick and dying. I could not cure them, no matter how hard I tried. So many threats to my village. People were raiding and killing one another. I could not protect them. Often there were food crises. I took more and more ebene to get assistance from the spirits, but my mind began to play tricks. Instead of help, my spirits left me with nothing but worry and fear. Sometimes I was so confused I wanted to escape into the forest, but I never ran off. Some men got lost in the spirit world when they took the drug; many ran into the jungle and were never heard from again. . . .

I wasn't strong enough to go on like this. A visitor from another village told me about foreign people, *nabas*, who had come to live on the river. [They] told me of a big spirit that could help us, one that was friendly and not desiring death and destruction. . . . When I stopped taking ebene and turned to the spirit of the nabas, I was happy to see that it was stronger than my forest spirits. They became afraid and went away. They didn't tell me to kill people or lead raids anymore. Instead, the new spirit told me to stop fights whenever I could."

A Yanomami man displays black face paint to show that he is in mourning for a dead relative.

and wildly pulling their hair. The hollow log with the unburned bones and teeth is then burned.

Finally, gourds containing the ashes are plugged and stored in the roof of the kin's *shabono*. They are later used in a second, more elaborate ash drinking ceremony involving kin from distant villages. At the second ceremony, large quantities of boiled plantain soup are prepared and the ashes are poured into gourds full of this soup. The gourds are passed around among the assembled close friends and relatives while the onlookers weep and mourn. After the ceremony a joyous feast is held.

Usually all the ashes are consumed. Important adults may have dozens of people partaking of their ashes, but children's ashes are eaten only by their parents. Men who have been killed by their enemies are given a special ritual. Their ashes are consumed only by women on the eve of a revenge raid. In this manner, the ashes of a man killed by his enemies may remain in the village for several years until the time is judged to be right for a raid.

Although the rites, rituals, and ceremonies of the Amazonians may seem strange to outsiders, they have been passed down through generations of the Yanomami for thousands of years. While modern people may think of the natives as a primitive people, the Yanomami spiritual world is extremely complicated and interwoven into every action of their daily lives.

Late Arrivals

C hristopher Columbus was the first European to visit Amazonia. When he sailed through the Orinoco River delta in 1498, he was so mesmerized by its beauty that he guessed that the source of the river must be in the biblical Garden of Eden. Soon after Columbus, Europeans invaded the area looking for the land of El Dorado—a place where there lived a mythical king so wealthy that he was said to be regularly showered with gold dust.

When Europeans first arrived in Amazonia in the early 1500s, the region was densely populated. The natives primarily lived along the rivers, as many still do today. In spite of the area's population, large tracts of its forest remained in their natural state, and the plants and animals needed for daily sustenance were in abundance.

Soon after the Europeans first explored the Amazon River, they drastically changed the region's culture and environment. Portuguese slave traders came to Amazonia and kidnapped whole tribes to sell into slavery. These raiders brought contagious diseases like cholera with them, to which the natives had little resistance. As a result, large numbers of natives died, leaving many areas abandoned.

The slave traders were followed by Jesuit missionaries who tried to "civilize" the natives by making them live and work in large farm communes. Although this form of servitude was considered a better alternative than slavery, the sixty Catholic compounds set up by the Jesuits in Amazonia banned the native languages, customs, and shamanic practices.

It was not until 1800 that a European, Alexander von Humboldt, first encountered a member of the Yanomami tribe. Despite having no close contact with them, he reported that they were a dangerous, warlike people. During the next century, as dozens of others pushed up the Orinoco searching for its

An illustration depicts Alexander von Humboldt encountering natives while traveling on the Orinoco River.

source, the reputation of the fierce Yanomami remained. However, these people managed to retain their indigenous worldview throughout the next five centuries of sporadic contact with outsiders.

The Rubber Boom

In the eighteenth century, explorers took rubber back to Europe, which led to a flourishing rubber trade. (The latex, or sap, from the rubber tree had already been used for centuries by the natives of the Amazon basin to waterproof their footwear and carrying bags.) Merchants who lived along the Amazon River began making annual expeditions up its tributaries to collect the latex from the various Indian communities, which were either persuaded or forced to supply it.

Then, around 1870, demand for rubber grew dramatically, setting off an Amazonian rubber boom. Traders brought outside rubber workers into the region, especially the rural poor fleeing droughts in northeastern Brazil. They cleared forests along the Amazon's tributaries, planted new rubber trees, and created a system of rubber plantations. This development led to harsh conditions for the indigenous people, who were forced into labor on the plantations or hunted down and killed. Those who were not exterminated had to retreat into the forest, away from the rivers.

Great wealth was created by the rubber boom, and large, modern cities grew up in the middle of the rain forest. Money for investment flowed in especially from British banks. Great rubber barons from the cities of Belém and Manaus controlled a network of rubber-estate owners (the *seringalistas*) and the masses of rubber tappers (the *seringueiros*), who were virtual slaves. Meanwhile, the nation of Brazil zealously guarded its monopoly on rubber, making it illegal to remove rubber-tree seedlings from the country.

In 1876 a British traveler smuggled rubber tree seedlings out of Brazil. The British government began planting rubber trees in Malaysia (in Southeast Asia), and by 1910 the Amazonian rubber boom collapsed. By the 1960s and 1970s the *seringalistas* abandoned their estates or sold them to ranchers. The 1980s saw a growing conflict between the ranchers, who wanted to clear the forest for pasture, and the rubber tappers, who still struggled to make a living by tapping Amazonian rubber trees.

Workers collect latex from Amazon rubber trees during the rubber boom of the late 1800s.

How the Amazon Got Its Name

In 1540 Francisco de Orellana launched an expedition east of the Andes Mountains to find the mythical gold of El Dorado in the Amazon rain forest. Orellana set out into the jungle with hundreds of soldiers, four thousand Indian slaves, two hundred horses, three thousand pigs, and packs of dogs trained to attack natives.

Orellana asked local natives the directions to El Dorado. When the natives could not answer, they were tortured and thrown to the ravenous hounds. Orellana eventually abandoned the group he set out with and ended up sailing alone down the entire stretch of the Amazon to the Atlantic Ocean. But he never found El Dorado. When asked to explain why he abandoned the others, Orellana claimed that his progress was impeded by savage Amazon women.

Orellana's excuse was based on the story called "The Amazons," which was written by the Greek writer Herodotus in 446 B.C. In Greek mythology, Amazons were a race of women warriors who only used men for creating children or fighting in battle. Likewise, Amazons raised only female children. Orellana imagined, sighted, or was attacked by female warriors. In reality he probably encountered Indian tribes where men and women fought side by side. In any event, Orellana's excuse gave the world's largest river its name.

Life of a Rubber Tapper

The traditional rubber estates operated on a system called debt bondage. During the rubber boom men who were rubber tappers were forbidden to grow their own food and were forbidden to marry. Likewise, they were obliged to sell their rubber to the estates at artificially low prices and to buy their food and tools at high prices at the estate store. These illiterate men were kept permanently in debt this way—and they were forced to eat nothing but canned food. Tappers were forbidden to leave the estate until the debt was paid off, which rarely happened.

This system loosened with the collapse of the rubber boom. Rubber tappers were allowed to grow subsistence crops and to hunt, although pressure remained to consume from the estate store.

Today this system continues to remain in place in many parts of the western Amazon.

The rubber tapper household is located in the forest. Each is separated by a walk of fifteen minutes to an hour. Behind each house, two or more looping trails pass up to two hundred naturally growing rubber trees.

The tapper's day starts before dawn, when he or she sets out on the trail. The tapper makes an incision in a tree and leaves a small cup to catch the latex that drips out. The day ends with the tapper transforming the liquid latex into a semisolid form. This is done either by pouring it onto a spit rotating over a smoky wood fire or by adding acetic acid (the sour, organic acid in vinegar or distilled wood) and pressing it into blocks.

Children learn to tap rubber at an early age. Although it is generally the men who do the tapping, women will also learn the skills. It is common for unmarried women to support their families by tapping rubber.

The late labor activist Chico Mendes writes of early life as a rubber tapper in the book *Fight for the Forest:*

Early Uses of Rubber

Europeans quickly adopted many uses for rubber after they discovered it in the eighteenth century. As early as the 1750s Portuguese merchants were sending army boots and knapsacks to Amazonia to be waterproofed with the native rubber. Even King José of Portugal sent his boots there for that purpose. By 1768 early scientists were making rubber tubing from the plant. A year later, an English chemist first erased pencil marks with what was then called India rubber.

In 1785 men first went aloft in rubber-coated balloons. A French rubber factory began producing ladies' garters in 1803. In 1811 the Champion company began rubber-coating boots for the French army. Charles Mackintosh discovered that naphtha added to rubber could be used to waterproof cloth and patented the process in 1823. (The British still call raincoats Mackintoshes or Macs.) The first rubber factory in the United States was opened in Roxbury, Massachusetts, in 1828. By 1839 a company was exporting 450,000 pairs of rubber shoes from Amazonia to New England. Prophylactics, made from Amazonian rubber, were first introduced in 1840.

The rubber trade in the Amazon changed drastically in 1844, when Charles Goodyear patented the means for making a stronger form of rubber. This process combined rubber and sulfur in the presence of heat—a process known as vulcanization. Super-tough vulcanized rubber goods could be used for making pneumatic (air-filled) tires and in heavy industrial processes such as mining, steel making, and other manufacturing.

A worker inspects a new tire at a Goodyear factory, named for the man whose ideas transformed the rubber trade.

My life began just like that of all rubber tappers, as a virtual slave bound to do the bidding of his master. I started working at nine years old, and like my father before me, instead of learning my ABCs I learned how to extract latex from a rubber tree. From the last century until 1970, schools were forbidden on any rubber estate in the Amazon. The rubber estate owners wouldn't allow it. . . . Because if a rubber tapper's children went to school, they would learn to read, write, and add up and would discover to what extent they were being exploited. . . .

So for many years, the great majority of us could neither read nor write. The rubber tapper worked all year hoping he would finally make a profit but always remained in debt. As he couldn't count, he couldn't tell whether he was being cheated or not.[19]

By the late 1980s environmentalists realized that saving the rubber tappers meant saving the Amazon rain forest. Extracting latex was an environmentally sound way to conserve forests and to provide jobs. Although the tapper's life was a hard one, it showed that people and the forest could coexist. Environmentalists set out to change the economic system that kept the tappers in poverty while preserving their important work in the forest.

Development Schemes and Highways

The rubber tappers were practically the only outsiders who worked in the jungle until the 1960s. But by 1964, Brazil was a land where 120 million people lived below the poverty line in large, filthy shantytowns. Amazonia was a roadless wilderness. This changed dramatically when Brazilian dictator Humberto de Alencar Castelo Branco initiated "Operation Amazonia" in 1966. The ill-conceived program, overseen by a corrupt military regime, was planned to open the Amazon to development.

Castelo Branco's government granted tax breaks, land concessions, trade agreements, sweetheart loans, and other credits to wealthy investors and corporations. Operation Amazonia was planned to develop commercial agriculture, mining, industry, and other enterprises in the Amazon. In addition, the plan would encourage immigration and settlement, develop roads, and exploit the region's timber and fishing resources. A special branch of the government, known as the Superintendency for the Amazonian Development (SUDAM), was put into place to oversee this expansion of the frontier.

Operation Amazonia originated when the government bulldozed a dirt highway east from Brasília—in the country's center—to Belém, an ancient port where the Amazon River meets the Atlantic Ocean. Ten years later, private construction companies worked with the military to cut a 1,875-mile swath through the jungle called the Transamazon Highway. Several other huge roads were slashed across the Brazilian rain forest, and land was cleared in 6-mile swaths on each side of the road. The total land used for these roads was 850,000 square miles—an area larger than all but eleven nations in the world. The new roads spurred an unprecedented land rush in Amazonia.

As part of the development scheme, the government reserved the six-mile stretch on either side of the Transamazon Highway for migrant families. The dreams of the settlers were

A bulldozer begins work in 1970 on the Transamazon Highway, a central feature of Brazil's Amazon development plan.

modest: a small plot of land, some cattle, and enough cash from farming to feed their families and buy a few modest possessions. Unfortunately, no one understood what the Yanomami had known for centuries: The soil of Amazonia will not support farms for more than a few years.

These projects created further problems unforeseen by SUDAM. Hundreds of primitive Indian tribes were suddenly thrown into contact with highway workers. Many natives died from the resulting diseases. The work of cutting the road was much more difficult than expected—some areas were too wet to support a road. Powerful new bulldozers and heavy equipment doubled the estimated cost of the highways.

The cleared land became ground zero for clashes between ranchers, rubber tappers, loggers, and miners—each fighting for a piece of a territory that rightfully belonged to the natives. Open war developed between wealthy ranchers, who ended up claiming most of the land, and landless peasants, or squatters, who illegally moved onto the land. What started out as a dreamland for peasants quickly became a region rife with violence and terrorism.

Cattle Ranches

By 1998 Brazil had slashed more than ninety-three hundred miles of railway lines and ninety-five hundred miles of roads into the vast ocean of forest. A tidal wave of settlers and developers quickly followed, leading to a landscape dominated by cattle pastures, ramshackled villages, pollution-spewing industries, and poverty-stricken farms.

Chico Mendes: Organizer of Rubber Tappers

Chico Mendes started tapping rubber trees at the age of nine. But, unlike other tappers, he learned to read and write. By the mid-1970s he organized a union to protect rubber tappers. At that time Mendes came into conflict with ranchers who wanted to clearcut the rain forest, destroying the land and the livelihood of the rubber tappers. In 1976 Mendes joined with a group of one hundred tappers to form a human chain between the forest and men wielding chain saws. They were severely beaten by police.

Mendes and other organizers soon formed a union of rubber tappers. It was a daunting task to organize people who lived in isolated pockets of the forest. Eventually, though, Mendes managed to bring the tappers together, along with the Indians, who were traditional enemies of the rubber workers who trespassed on their native lands.

By 1987 Mendes claimed to have saved 3 million acres of rain forest from the chain saws. But the agreements worked out between the landowners, the land-grabbers, and the rubber tappers were not particularly successful. Ranchers offered tappers small areas of land or money to leave. The tappers steadfastly refused because they could not live on the pittance offered. This position outraged the ranchers and state officials; they reacted by hiring gunmen to assassinate union organizers.

On December 22, 1988, Chico Mendes stood on the steps of his house in the town of Xapuri. He was killed by a blast of lead from a .20 gauge shotgun at a distance of about twenty-five feet. Since that time, Mendes has become a martyr to the thousands of people who are working to save the rain forests.

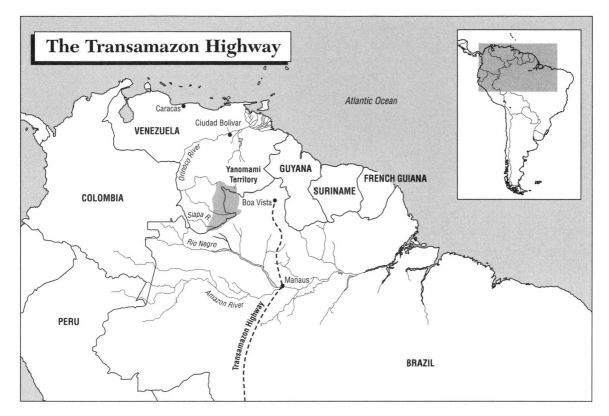

The Transamazon Highway

To understand Brazil's economy, it is important to know that 2 percent of the people in Brazil control 60 percent of the land. Close to 70 percent of the poor families have no property. The estates controlled by the wealthy are enormous. Only 340 ranchers in Amazonia control a total of 183,000 square miles—an area larger than the state of California. In an area with no police or justice system, many of the landholdings are expanded by fake titles and outright theft. Ranchers also use slave labor and debt bondage to control workers; this area has one of the worst human rights records in Brazil.

The government's main incentive for turning the forest into cattle ranches was the demand for beef fueled by Brazil's swelling population. Eighty-five percent of the land cleared was populated by livestock, but few of these farms lasted much longer than a tradi-tional Yanomami garden. After ten years at the most, the cow pastures lost their fertility and became choked by certain weeds that are toxic to cattle. The hoofbeats of the cows also made the land an easy target for erosion and fire. Ranchers burned the fields and the nutrient-rich ash kept the fields marginally productive for a few years. Before long, however, the pastures quit producing enough edible grass to support cows. Then, other huge tracts of land were cut and burned.

Most ranches last less then five years in Amazonia, and all the ranches carved into the forest before 1978 were gone by 1985, overtaken by rough scrub. These farms did not deliver the riches envisioned by early backers of Operation Amazonia, but the tax incentives and subsidies provided by the government did make people wealthy even while their ranches went broke. In spite of this dismal

Ramshackle villages dot the countryside along highways built under Operation Amazonia.

economic and environmental record, large banks continued to pump billions into ranches in the rain forest.

Ecologists point out that ranching is the least efficient way to use the forest. To make a million dollars ranching, a person needs to cut down 38 square miles of forest; to make the same amount of money logging, a person only needs to cut less than 1 square mile; to make that much surface mining, a mere 0.0006 square miles.

Besides cattle ranching, large tracts of Amazonia have also been divided into gigantic plantations for palm oil, cocoa, coffee, tea, sugarcane, bananas, and other export crops.

Life on the Ranch

While some Amazonian ranches are owned by faraway cattle barons, many small-time operators tough it out on tropical cattle ranches; and the daily life of an average rancher is hardly glamorous. Cowboys live in small ranch houses cluttered with hammocks, hats, rifles, saddles, liquor bottles, and cigarette butts. Outhouses dot the landscape, and bathrooms

with running water are scarce. Kitchens are full of blackened pots where rice, beans, onions, and coffee are prepared. Sacks of bug-infested maniocs compete for space with hanging dried meat and curing hides.

Poor people who become ranchers have to clear their land with chain-saw gangs because heavy equipment is too expensive. Once the trees are cut, the land is burned. Grass is planted and constant attention must be paid to weeding. Some ranchers spray herbicides from airplanes while others use teams of laborers to weed. The pasture is worthless after a few years, and fertilizer does not help; it is cheaper to simply cut and burn a new area.

When English author Binka Le Breton asked a small-time rancher about the mass burning of the forest, the rancher replied, "There's been a lot of fuss lately about burning the forest, but everyone knows that it's the First World (industrialized countries), not us, that's responsible for the greenhouse effect. It's the carbon emissions from all their cars." [20]

Many small ranchers were ignorant of the fact that anyone previously lived on the land they now claimed, and they were surprised to come into conflict with rubber tappers, who they thought were driven out decades ago. When tappers protest the logging, they are usually met with strong-arm tactics. One rancher gives his views on the tappers:

> I offered [the tappers] plots of land elsewhere. . . . But they didn't want *those* plots; said that there wasn't enough rubber, and that each family needed 450 to 750 acres. Where . . . was I going to put my cattle?

> And then they started this business of "peaceful protests." They're a bunch of communists, if you ask me. They'd get a whole gang of people together, including women and children, and they'd walk in and frighten off my workers. . . . There's people trying to make out that Chico Mendes was some sort of saint. He was nothing more than a nuisance, a communist agitator. . . . It was a great waste of time, particularly as I . . . always ended up clearing the forest anyway.[21]

Ranchers in general—and wealthy ones in particular—do not like foreigners and journalists investigating their huge estates or business practices. Some have been on the land for decades, and they take pride in having "settled" the wilderness. Most of them could not make a living anywhere else.

Logging

Tropical forests provide about one-fifth of all wood used worldwide. Demand for tropical hardwoods has soared in recent years. Prized for strength, color, and resistance to decay, hardwoods are found in a variety of items, including furniture, musical instruments, plywood, house siding, salad bowls, and lawn furniture. Many of these one-thousand-year-old trees are cut down to make cheap plywood that is used only once for concrete forms in building construction.

Loggers claim that when the ranchers clear the land, hundreds of millions of dollars

Cattle graze amid the remains of a burned-out section of the Amazon rain forest.

worth of wood goes up in smoke. The wood is burned because there is a labor shortage— not enough men to cut the wood down. Waste is also rampant when dozens of species of trees are knocked down without being used. The international market only requires wood it knows—cedar, mahogany, jacaranda, and virola. Rosewood is nearly extinct, and other species are simply left to rot.

After roads were built through the jungles, the loggers were quick to follow. Mill towns have sprung up here and there along the roads. Many are haphazard collections of wooden shacks that are linked together by muddy tracks through the bush. Long lines of log-laden trucks inch through the towns, spewing diesel smoke. Sawmills are located near the edges of towns, where mammoth stacks of mahogany and other hardwoods are piled up. Each log has a girth as great as a man's height.

The big logs are first sliced sideways. The sliced wood is placed flat on trolleys and is then sawed into planks. Much of the wood is wasted and lies about in piles. It is eventually burned, leaving a gray pall of smoke over the landscape.

The workers are not ready to give up their jobs for ecological reasons, as one mill owner makes clear:

You want to know where this [wood] comes from? It comes from the Suruí Indians. They've got plenty more in there. I get their wood. The chief gets a pickup truck and a parabolic antenna for his television. Everyone's happy.

These forests were given to us by God to be used. I go in there, I get out the good trees, I move on. . . . Mind you, there's some countries where they want to ban the import of tropical hardwoods altogether. The ones that are endangered, that is. Can you imagine anything so silly? Do that, and there'll be no point having forests at all. After all, if they're worth something, people will take the trouble to look after them.

When asked about replanting the forests, the logger answered:

Sawmills like this one in the Amazon rain forest help fill the world's ever-increasing demand for wood.

Miners dig for gold at Serra Pelada in Brazil during the gold rush of the 1980s. The influx of gold miners has devastated the rain forest.

No, reforestation isn't my business. When I'm through, the landowner will go in there and burn the place over, and then he'll turn it into pasture. He can't afford to even think of reforesting. He's not going to be around in fifty years when those trees come in. Mind you, there *are* people looking into the question. It ought to be done. But it's not my job. We've got to look after ourselves here and now, haven't we?[22]

Government bureaucracy also works against replanting. A higher monetary value is placed on cleared land than forestland. Clearing is regarded as an improvement; if someone clears a piece of land, his title to it is ensured. From the loggers' point of view, it is better to cut and run. Markets are uncertain, currency values fluctuate, and Brazil's economic stability is nonexistent.

The Work of Gold Miners

The first satellite photographs of Amazonia were made by the Brazilian Radar Institute in the 1960s. On Yanomami lands, they detected large deposits of gold and cassiterite, the latter an extremely valuable mineral used to make tin. There is an estimated 11,000 tons of gold, or 11 percent of the world's supply, in the Orinoco River basin. There are also huge deposits of iron ore, diamonds, and bauxite (the principal ore used in aluminum). On the north shore of the Orinoco a reserve of extra-heavy crude oil is estimated at more than 270 billion barrels. (To put this in perspective, in 1997 the United States consumed approximately 6.4 billion barrels of oil.)

In the 1980s the availability of light-weight, inexpensive aircraft and advances in satellite photography renewed interest in

Gold miners who sought riches in mines found on Yanomami land are evicted.

mining this formerly inaccessible region. Tens of thousands of frontier miners were anxious to claim the minerals before large corporations stepped in. Some of the richest gold veins were on land most densely populated by the Yanomami. In their quest for riches, the miners gave little thought to the natives, whom they viewed as mere obstacles to either be ignored or killed.

When the miners invaded traditional Yanomami communities, disease ran rampant among the natives. In 1980 a planeload of miners infected a Yanomami village with measles; twenty-seven natives died. Missionaries and scientists protested the invasion, medical teams were sent to the area, and the miners were forced to leave.

In 1984 a presidential decree gave mining companies the right to prospect on Indian lands. By 1989 the miners' occupation of Indian lands was an established fact. Romero Juca, the governor of the state where the mining took place, backed the miners. He said it would be easier for the smaller amount of Yanomami Indians to "be put onto a reservation instead of taking out the forty-five thousand miners who are already there."[23]

Gold mining wreaks havoc on the fragile lands of Amazonia. Instead of digging up the earth, miners use high-pressure water hoses to simply spray away the soft, pliant rain for-est soil while searching for minerals underneath. According to filmmaker and author Geoffrey O'Connor,

> The Yanomami [were forced to] come to terms with the sheer numbers of the white man, a strange people who by the tens of thousands descend to earth in giant metal birds (airplanes) and who employ noisy machines to carry them everywhere, to bring light to their houses, to give energy to the orange hoses and hydraulic pumps tearing apart the once pristine riverbanks of this part of the forest. (The Yanomami refer to the miners as "wild pigs snorting in the mud" because of the way they press their bodies into the sides of the rivers as they search the embankments for gold.)[24]

The gold miners are supported by crowds of merchants who supply food, fuel, supplies, and radio transmissions into the forest.

The Work of Mining

Like other Amazonian enterprises, gold mining ventures are dominated by a few bosses who rule over their mining claims like dictators. Poor, illiterate workers labor relentlessly in the searing sun, humidity, and mud. There are no laws and no police. Murder among the miners is common and accidents are rampant.

Solemn, weary miners wear shorts, T-shirts, and hiking boots, and they carry huge lengths of orange rubber hoses. They call themselves *formigas*, or ants, but they are another generation of South American peasants chasing the dream of riches. The minerals lie in the embankments of the snakelike rivers that twist and turn through the rain forest on their way to the mighty Amazon. The fat, orange hoses, powered by shrieking Yamaha electric generators, spray the mud from the riverbanks. The mud is washed into filtration tanks where the minerals are screened out.

Geoffrey O'Connor describes this type of mining as

> all part of the age-old business of sifting through the earth in the hope of discovering precious metals. . . . Here it is as if the Medieval Age and the Industrial Age have suddenly become fused: paradise for those who own the mine but purgatory for those who are forced to work in them.[25]

From where the miners stand, the scene looks like a devastated lunar crater. Everything is covered with light brown mud that splatters from the hose pressure. Large trees topple over as the soil beneath them is washed away. The tiny, powerful generators vibrate constantly on wooden platforms and give off a deafening noise as they drive the hydraulic pumps. O'Connor depicts the workers like this:

> A miner, eyes vacant, covered in dirt from head to toe, slowly wades past through a pool of water, showing no recognition of our presence. This is the land of the walk-

ing wounded, a mud-caked hell on earth where men are so far beyond the point of exhaustion that a simple hello is visibly difficult. Most of them just blink at you as if a wave or gesture entails too much effort in this dreadful heat. . . .

> The miners who control the hoses seem to be in a hypnotic trance as they twist and turn, their bodies wrestling the blast of the jet spray.[26]

Above this scene, bosses stand in the unmined areas in clean clothes, looking on and jotting on clipboards. They are the ones who originally discovered the sites. They purchased the equipment and brought each miner to the forest at a cost of eight hundred dollars, which is taken out of each man's share of the profits. The bosses take 70 percent of the profits while the workers split the remaining 30 percent. The workers must buy food, supplies, and medicine at the company store at prices that are five times what they would be in the nearest town.

This type of life is extremely difficult for the miners, but as in other business ventures in the forest, the Yanomami and other natives are the real losers. Besides the diseases carried by the miners, in 1993 miners murdered fourteen native men, women, and children in a remote village. Other unsolved murders of Indians occur on a regular basis.

The Yanomami can barely comprehend the resource-hungry world that is the final destination of the logs, minerals, meat, and rubber that come from their homeland. But it has become a fact of life that commerce is here to stay in the rain forest. Its effects on the natives who still follow traditions forged ten thousand years ago has not been positive.

Outside Influences

Although the Yanomami periodically clashed with outsiders, Amazonia's population of whites in the seventeenth, eighteenth, and nineteenth centuries remained sparse. Major urban centers never contained more than one hundred thousand people. That changed, however, as the centuries passed.

The Yanomami did not experience sustained contact with outsiders until 1910. At that time the presence of outsiders forced the Yanomami into contact with religious missionaries and Brazil's Indian Protection Service. The missionaries navigated up the intricate waterways in small, light boats that they carried around the many waterfalls. The missionaries were followed by traders, whose products were enough to draw several Yanomami communities closer to the river. These Indians sought items that could be bartered with others farther back in the forest. The Yanomami especially valued machetes and axes used to clear gardens. Despite these points of contact, the Yanomami had only brief interaction with small numbers of whites.

By the 1950s, however, the increased presence of outsiders could no longer be ignored by the Indians. The Yanomami called them "the real foreigners," or *kraiwa*, "the white people." Their numbers and plans were still unclear, but the *kraiwa* arrived by canoes and airplanes and were generally friendly.

The outsiders were white missionaries, anthropologists, and government employees who arrived in large numbers by the early 1960s. The Indians believed these strangers to be communicating with each other by using the same supernatural songs that their shamans used. They would watch the white people talk all day into boxes called two-way radios. One person would speak, then a voice would come out of the box. To the Yanomami, it only made sense that the whites used the same method of communication that they used. With time, however, the Yanomami understood the way two-way radios functioned.

But life went on as it always had for most of the sixteen thousand Yanomami who still lived in the southern Venezuelan state of Amazonas. Although they adopted some of the modern technologies from visitors—steel fishhooks, rifles, and axes—some are thirsting for more from the outside world.

The Influence of Missionaries

Missionaries have attempted to convert natives to Christianity for centuries. Competing religious groups each try to put forth their brand of religion, often causing conflict. Like all other contact with outsiders, this conversion came to the Yanomami only in recent decades. With the arrival of the Rio Negro and Roman Catholic missions, the Protestant Evangelical Amazonic Mission, and New Tribes of Brazil in the 1960s, the Yanomami came into contact with mainstream society and their population ceased to grow.

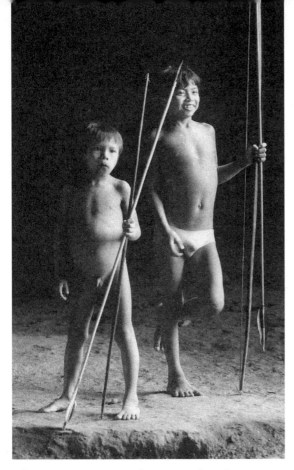

Christian missionaries have introduced many changes in Yanomami culture, including the wearing of underwear.

An example of what can happen when the Yanomami mix with outsiders was seen in 1987. At that time a group of Yanomami were enticed to abandon their traditional *shabono* to live near a Salesian Catholic missionary village on the Mavaca River (a tributary of the Orinoco River). Here, the Yanomami lived in three-cornered *yanos*, temporary huts normally used while camping in the forest. The new contact exposed them not only to missionaries but also to young men with shotguns and motorboats who harassed the Yanomami for sport.

The Yanomami had cleared and planted a huge garden at the new site, but at the urging of the missionaries they planted it all with only one crop—manioc. This crop usually takes up only 10 percent of a traditional garden, but a Salesian brother had urged them to plant it exclusively so they could sell the mission the manioc flour that they would make on new machines provided by the mission.

The missionaries had constructed a school even before the Yanomami could build a *shabono*. It was a large open hut with a gabled roof, and it was full of tables and chairs. The teacher stocked the shelves with food to entice children into the class. The food was oatmeal, rice, milk, sugar, and salt. These seemingly harmless items—especially the sugar—make the usually cavity-free teeth of the Yanomami rot and fall out. And it did not take long before fights broke out over the unguarded food; one young man was even beaten to death over accusations of school food theft.

By 1992 an epidemic swept through the village of 164 people. Twenty-one died in one week, most of them males, including several legendary headmen. The missionaries, though aware of the outbreak, sent no one to aid the sick and dying. Anthropologist Napoleon A. Chagnon blames this outbreak on the huge amount of trash and pollution that had been dumped in the river by outsiders. This pollution consisted of broken glass, food waste, tin cans, outboard motors, sheet-metal roofing, and other waste.

The Influence of Outside Education

The children of the Salesian village began to regularly attend school in the late 1980s. They even had a school bus—a large dugout canoe—that picked up children from twelve villages every morning and returned them at night. School deeply affected the traditional Yanomami lifestyle. Chagnon reports of asking a village headman when he planned on leaving on an extended food-gathering trip. The reply: "We will go gathering during the school vacation break."[27] The anthropologist also heard the Yanomami making plans for the weekend or when school was out. Coming from a primitive people who never had clocks or calendars, Chagnon writes, "I still find it difficult to hold a straight face when a Yanomami refers to 'the weekend,' even at a mission post."[28]

Educated Yanomami quickly adopt Spanish (the language of Venezuela) and Portuguese (the language of Brazil). They also learn to read and write in Spanish, Portuguese, and Yanomaman. (Although Yanomaman is not a written language, linguists and anthropologists have converted the spoken language into written form.) Some individuals become remarkably literate.

Along with education comes the other trappings of civilization. Young Yanomami men were heard conversing about the latest Hollywood action movie they had seen at the mission. And those aren't the only types of movies shown—soldiers in the area have been known to show the Yanomami pornographic movies as well.

The Influence of Encroaching Civilization

The accelerated destruction of the Amazon rain forest directly affects those indigenous peoples who rely on the forest for their livelihoods. Hamo Opikteri, a Yanomami Indian who lives in Brazil's Catrimani Valley, discusses this problem:

> Everyone will come here and will finish off with everything, with game, fish, with pigs, with everything that we use to sustain ourselves. You will contaminate, you will bring a lot of sicknesses, a lot of malaria, sicknesses we have never seen, that we never have suffered. Because, without the white man, we never suffered from the sicknesses that people have suffered today.[29]

Yanomami children show fascination for items not found in their traditional way of life.

A group of Yanomami Indians begs at a mining camp airstrip.

When the forest is destroyed, the plants and animals that natives depend on are also destroyed. Deforestation in Amazonia is caused by both frontier expansion and internationally financed development projects. When land-hungry settlers invade, they purposefully settle on Indian lands. Then, the settler's rights to the land are guaranteed by government-sponsored colonization programs.

When Indians lose control of their natural resources, they become impoverished and homeless. They migrate toward regional towns and cities where they are condemned to a wretched future of unemployment, begging, homelessness, prostitution, and disease. Obtaining enough fish and game becomes impossible for these refugees.

Author Geoffrey O'Connor describes a group of Yanomami women near a mining camp airstrip:

The women's clothes are dirty and torn, the once colorful patterns of their dresses are now indistinguishable under the layer of grime that covers them. They are probably hand-me-downs given by missionaries who used to occupy this airstrip, or maybe they were gained in a trade for bananas or corn with some local miners. The women, small in stature like most of the Yanomami, all appear to be in their twenties. They have strong arms, large muscular shoulders, and sturdy legs. According to what I have read, they can deftly handle an ax or trek twenty miles through the forest in a single day. Their lives are spent cultivating the gardens, fetching hefty baskets of firewood, and toting water jugs from nearby rivers and streams. All of this work is done while they tend to their children, very often carrying infants in tree-bark slings as they go about their tasks. . . . The eyes of the women . . . shift about as if they expect to be struck at any moment. . . .

Providing Medical Care

All humans have antibodies to protect them from various diseases. In 1967 researchers determined that the Yanomami have no antibodies against measles. This indicated that they had never been exposed to this highly contagious disease. In 1968 the researchers brought vaccines against measles to the Yanomami, but an epidemic hit exactly at the same time. Thirty to 40 percent of people in some villages died from measles; those who were vaccinated survived.

In recent years a group of Venezuelan doctors have formed a voluntary group to minister to the medical needs of the Yanomami. These doctors fight against harsh terrain, lack of funds, superstitions, and ignorance about contagious diseases. But even in this endeavor there is the question of how much outsiders should do for rural tribes. Napoleon A. Chagnon addresses this issue in his book *Yanomamö: The Last Days of Eden*.

"The basic medical dilemma is this: Should the Yanomami who have not been directly contacted [by outsiders] be left alone? Or should we go into those areas to provide medical services . . . ? The first option could ultimately result in devastating epidemics and predictable decimation of the population. The second option would increase outside contact and speed the rate of cultural exchange.

Is there a middle ground? The only one I can think of is a kind of compromise in which the remotest villages have the option of becoming involved in the process of cultural change or of remaining aloof from it."

A traveling team of Brazilian health workers checks for malaria among the members of a remote Yanomami tribe.

Begging has now become part of life for these women, a chore that they have learned to incorporate into their daily routines. . . . The scenes of begging I've witnessed . . . confirm the worst fears of health officials in the cities: malnutrition will go hand in hand with malaria in decimating this once healthy Indian population.[30]

There are still vast areas of reality and experience that the Yanomami cannot share with white people. There is a twenty-thousand-year gap in the culture's worldview that cannot be easily bridged. Differences in language and culture cause many often fatal problems. For instance, in 1996 a Yanomami man shot and killed two miners near an airstrip. No one knows what caused this violence. In retaliation, a group of miners abducted and killed four Indians. They mutilated their bodies and left them on the airstrip not far from a Yanomami village. This act was calculated to terrorize the natives, who abhor blood and mistreatment of the dead. Forever after, when the Indians were forced to cross the airstrip they were almost paralyzed with fear. Their faces were locked in horrific grimaces whenever any white people approached them.

The Influence of Rock Stars and Social Activists

Of course, not all outsiders come to Amazonia to harm the Yanomami. In the late 1980s, as the plight of the Indians spread to the outside world, dozens of organizations were formed with the goal of helping the Yanomami and the rain forest survive. One of the most famous people to become involved with the cause was rock musician Sting.

When Sting traveled to the Amazon he attracted large crowds of photographers, reporters, and fans, just as he did elsewhere. Geoffrey O'Connor writes about one of Sting's 1989 press conferences:

"I spent a day yesterday with some Kayapo in the jungle and realized that I was in Paradise," says Sting. "That I was in the Garden of Eden." He pauses, takes a . . . breath, and continues.

"If that culture is destroyed, then the world will lose something that is invaluable," he says. "I also think that by saving the Indians, you save the rain forest. They are the gardeners of the forest. So we have to protect them to protect the forest. . . ."

"I am here to speak for my own people. . . . We want to help save the rain forest. We want to try and declare a huge National Park at the center of the Amazon. We need funds to do it. We need a few million dollars. . . ."

Rock musician Sting, who was inspired to save the rain forests by the Kayapo Indians, holds a news conference with a tribal chief.

The rock star rambles on for another fifteen minutes, giving details of his plans to establish boundaries around part of Kayapo land known as Menkragnoti territory. . . . A worldwide tour has been planned . . . to get the message out. He peppers his statements with assurances that his new foundation will be working "with" Brazilians, that this is "a Brazilian initiative," that it won't be like "North Americans trying to tell the Brazilians what to do."[31]

Since that time Sting and his wife, Trudie Styler, have headed the Rainforest Foundation International (RFI), which was the first organization to advocate the twin needs of protecting both the rain forest and the cultures that rely on it. Sting was inspired to start the RFI by Raoni, a chief of the Menkragnoti Kayapó who made a simple plea: help him protect his homeland in Brazil from being devastated by gold mining and logging activities. To raise money, the RFI has produced star-studded annual benefit concerts featuring pop stars such as Elton John, Bonnie Raitt, Stevie Wonder, James Taylor, Lyle Lovett, Bobby McFerrin, Shawn Colvin, Emmylou Harris, and others.

The mission of the RFI is to support indigenous peoples and traditional populations of the rain forest in their efforts to protect their environment. The foundation helps natives secure and control natural resources and manage the resources in ways that do not harm the environment.

Four years later, the goal was achieved as the RFI helped pass legislation that protects seventeen thousand square miles of rain forest.

Upholding the Rights of the Natives

The government of Brazil grants Indians a legal right to permanent possession of their lands. Under Article 231 of the 1988 Brazilian constitution, the indigenous people have an inalienable right to their ancestral lands and

Drinking, Drugs, and Prostitution

Traditional Yanomami shamans have long used drugs in their spiritual ceremonies. Young men are taught to use the drugs by older men, and the use of drugs is strictly regulated by tradition. But like the diseases of the civilized world, alcohol and addictive drugs like cocaine have taken their toll on the Yanomami. Men of the tribes go to nearby mining towns and logging camps where they become drunk and disorderly, and morally bankrupt drug dealers use the Yanomami to help them smuggle drugs through rural areas.

Dislocation and poverty have also forced some Yanomami women to turn to prostitution as a means of survival. The invasion of gold miners is blamed as the principal cause of this problem. The miners often give women food in exchange for sexual favors, while their husbands might be offered weapons. Prostitution has fueled an increase in venereal diseases and AIDS among the Yanomami—whose resistance to such diseases is low.

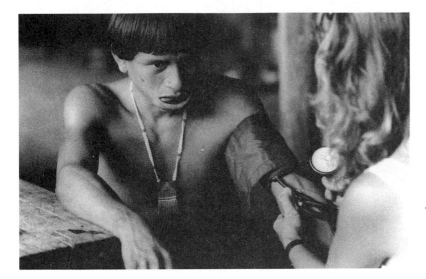

A Yanomami man is examined by a medical worker from the Commission for the Creation of a Yanomami Reserve, one of many groups trying to help natives regain control of their ancestral lands.

natural resources. The constitution also guarantees their right to exist as a distinct culture. In 1991 Decree 22 strengthened the constitution by granting Indians primary rights over competing interests, such as gold miners, ranchers, and loggers.

But considerations of national security and development sometimes take precedence over those rights. In 1996 Brazil's president signed Decree 1775 into law. Decree 1775 has been dubbed the "genocide decree" by human rights activists because it allows commercial interests to protest indigenous land titles and undermines the rights of Indians to their traditional territories as guaranteed in Brazil's 1988 constitution. It also takes the control of natural resources—which local communities depend on for survival—out of native hands. In the end, the words on Brazil's constitution have done little to protect the natives.

After Decree 1775 was passed, commercial interests immediately began to reverse indigenous land titles. The farming conglomerate Agropecuaria Sattin was the first to act, contesting the native Guarani-Kaiowa territory of Sete Cerros in the Brazilian state of Mato Grosso do Sul. Pirate mahogany loggers and gold miners have taken Decree 1775 as a sign of government sanction and have quickly moved their operations onto Indian lands. At least eight Indian areas were invaded in the weeks after the decree was signed.

Decree 1775 also opened previously restricted areas to development, including the gold-rich lands of the Yanomami. In response, the Yanomami held an assembly to organize resistance to politicians and economic interests, decrying the devastating effects of continued invasion by gold miners who pollute the rivers and forests as well as introduce disease. At the present time, a tug of war between the government, the indigenous tribes, and various commercial interests is far from resolution.

Caught in a Political Crossfire

The government is run by politicians and, unfortunately for the indigenous people of the Amazon, politics are controlled by the rich and powerful. Yanomami lands are legally

The Cause of Malaria

Since 1987 nearly 25 percent of the Yanomami population has been wiped out by diseases carried by the unwanted colonists. The main killer is malaria, which is spread by the deadly anopheles mosquitoes that breed in the large stagnant ponds left behind by the gold miners. But the Yanomami might be contributing to their own destruction as well. Geoffrey O'Connor explains the situation in his *Amazon Journal:*

"[The ponds] are common sights when flying over Yanomami territory today: hundreds of large gold pits filled with water stand out like massive blemishes in what would otherwise be lush green forest. The pits are mined, but abandoned as the prospectors move on in search of other gold deposits. The construction of a hundred new airstrips by gold prospectors in just two years has also drastically multiplied the potential breeding area for the Anopheles.

However, this is not a one-dimensional story. Placing the blame is more complicated. The Yanomami might also unknowingly be contributing to their own demise. Many villages, attracted by the prospect of trading goods, have in recent years started moving closer to the rivers, placing their people in contact with groups of outsiders, as well as pools of stagnant water, thereby increasing the possibility of infection. With the machetes obtained by trading, [the Yanomami] have begun to clear larger plots for villages and gardens. Those in turn become expanded breeding grounds for mosquitoes."

Malnutrition and malaria have wiped out nearly 25 percent of the Yanomami population since 1987.

protected, but it has been almost impossible to keep gold miners from seeking their fortune in Yanomami territory.

Although the mining is illegal, in 1996 the Brazilian government suspended the helicopter surveillance operations in the area that were designed to thwart the miners. Since that time, thousands of gold prospectors reinvaded the Yanomami area in northern Brazil. The result has been a dramatic rise in malaria cases and the deaths of dozens of Indians who were shot by gold miners. Thirty-five illegal airstrips were put into operation to supply the miners, and a government-sponsored health organization, the Pro-Yanomami Commission (CCPY), has been threatened by insufficient funding. The government of Venezuela has a stricter protection program, but this has only led to an exodus of gold miners crossing into Yanomami territory on the Brazilian side of the border.

Ranchers also use politics to lay claim to native lands. In 1994, in Mato Grosso do Sul,

700 Guarani Indians had moved back to their homeland after they were evicted from the area in the 1970s. The 108 families who returned, built homes and planted crops.

In 1996 the Guarani were ordered off their lands by a local judge. The Indians, he said, were "invaders" who were illegally occupying land that belonged to ranchers.

The Guarani number twenty-five thousand, making them Brazil's largest group of indigenous people. But social problems

Though mining is not as heavy as it was in the 1980s, its effects still threaten the Amazon rain forest.

caused by a lack of land have driven many to alcoholism and suicide. After the families were evicted, the natives went back to court in an attempt to secure title to their homeland.

Venezuela's Rain Forest Opens to Mining

Nearly half of Venezuela is covered with pristine tropical rain forest. This vast area, called the Imataca Forest Reserve is one of the four largest forest reserves in Venezuela. Its total area is 360 million acres—nearly as large as Switzerland. The area has been a government-protected reserve for the past thirty years. Part of this territory is also home to five indigenous groups—the Warrau, Arawak, Karina, Akawaio, and Pemon—who have inhabited the area for centuries and whose survival depends on the surrounding natural environment. But the Imataca sits on enormous underground reserves of gold and diamonds. In 1997 the Venezuelan government, deep in debt, decided to tap this reserve to promote economic development.

For years the area had been invaded by illegal gold miners. By the end of 1996 almost 10 percent of Imataca was subject to mining in this way. But these vast reserves have caught the attention of international mining companies. In May 1997 the government decided to carve up the area between mining firms and logging companies. They ignored the protected status of the forest, ignored the rights of the indigenous peoples who lived there, and ignored the national and international agreements on indigenous rights and environmental protection. The agreements left less than 4 percent of the forest protected. The hastily passed law to allow this was called Government Decree 1850. This law plainly contradicts dozens of previous laws that were passed to protect the region.

National protests by indigenous groups, environmentalists, and social groups challenged the plan in court. The Venezuelan Supreme Court is currently investigating legal cases brought by environmental and indige-

Problems with Mercury

To extract gold from river sediment, mercury is used in two distinct phases of the mining process. First, the sediment is passed through a sieve. Mercury is then placed into the sieved sediment that helps coagulate the gold. During this process a certain amount of mercury spills into the river. The second phase involves burning off the mercury, which is highly toxic, to leave behind the gold. The burned mercury evaporates into the atmosphere, but it comes back down into the rivers and streams during rainstorms.

Researchers have discovered that an alarming 100 percent of the Amazon's Indians show dangerous levels of mercury in their blood and urine samples. The highest levels occurred in villages where the diet was mainly fish.

Mercury poisoning may corrode people's skin and mucous membranes. If it is inhaled into the lungs it can cause severe pneumonia and even death. Chronic mercury poisoning like that occurring in the Amazon can result in various cancers and dementia.

Forest fires rage out of control in Amazonia in March 1998.

nous groups and by the Congressional Commission on the Environment, which claims the plan is illegal under Venezuelan law.

Fires in the Rain Forest

The weather systems of the world are interconnected, and they change constantly from year to year. The Yanomami might feel that they live at the center of the universe, but their environment can be harmed by global weather trends as well as the felling of the forests in their own backyard. This point was clearly demonstrated in March 1998 when a wave of forest fires swept through Amazonia.

For two months fires burned precious rain forest that had been untouched by loggers. The fires threatened the Yanomami in northern Brazil. The forest is usually too wet to burn, but the fires were blamed on the El Niño weather phenomenon that caused a long drought. The fires burned about 22,000 square miles, an area slightly larger than the nation of Costa Rica. The fires threatened the 25-million-acre reservation that is home to 9,000 Yanomami Indians. The smoke from the fires closed nearby airports, grounding airplanes and helicopters needed to fight the fire. Although at least 1,000 firefighters were needed, only 250 were available. When fires reached Indian villages, farmers were forced to fight them by beating the flames with blankets and sticks.

At the end of March, the first strong rains in six months helped put out the flames of the raging conflagration. These rains came one day after two Kayapó Indian shamans were flown to the Yanomami reservation to perform a special ritual they believed would bring rain. The ritual involved dancing, praying, and the gathering of leaves. The rains quenched 80 to 90 percent of the fires. Whether this was a coincidence or real Yanomami magic depends on the viewpoint of the observer. Whatever the case, experts called the fires an unprecedented environmental disaster.

Forest fires, missionaries, rock stars, politicians, and gold miners are some of the outside influences that have changed the lives of natives of Amazonia. The Yanomami have little control over elections, illegal mining and logging, and weather patterns that may have been altered by industrial nations. The savvy among the natives employ rock stars like Sting to tell the world about their cause, but despite the efforts of those who want to help, there seems to be no end to the outside influences invading Yanomami lands.

Survival in a Changing World

People living in the modern world must make a giant leap of the imagination to understand the natives of Amazonia. They must forget their high-tech world of cars and computers to peer deep into an environment of plants, animals, and untouched rivers. Few are willing to make this leap, and so the Yanomami and other tribes are faced with the task of surviving in the modern world. Various plans and programs have been put into place to help indigenous people survive in today's global economic system.

Because of the well-publicized gold rush of 1987, the plight of the Yanomami became well-known. This set into motion a competition among environmental and human rights groups to help or direct the Yanomami. These groups consist of anthropologists, survivalists, conservation activists, government agencies, and even the United Nations. Each wants to institute its own plan to save the Yanomami from civilization; each adopts potential Yanomami leaders to carry its message. As Napoleon A. Chagnon writes,

> Now that the Yanomami are famous, they seem to be a commodity that interest groups are competing for. . . . A major stimulus for the competition is the high visibility of the Yanomami as a symbol of the plight of all indigenous peoples, especially those in the Amazon, and of the efforts to conserve the world's biodiversity and its tropical forests.[32]

Working for the Indians

The politics of saving Amazonia are as complicated and interwoven as the plant and animal species in the forest itself. As the Kayapó Indian leader Paiakan points out,

> The forest is one big thing; it has people, animals, and plants. There is no point saving the animals if the forest is burned down; there is no point saving the forest if the people and animals who live in it are killed and driven away. The groups trying to save the race of animals cannot win if the people trying to save the forest lose; the people trying to save the Indians cannot win if either of the others lose; the Indians cannot win without the support of these groups; but the groups cannot win without the help of the Indians, who know the forest and the animals and can tell what is happening to them. No one of us is strong enough to win alone; together, we can be strong enough to win.[33]

Still, Yanomami leaders themselves—both new and old—must make important decisions for their people. They have to decide which outsiders are friends and which are foes, and they must analyze conflicting information, lies, and rumors that are circulated among them.

Complex information reaches the Yanomami through mission posts. Some natives are able to interpret it better than others, but as the information is passed along to remote

A tranquil Amazon River scene at sunset represents a way of life that may soon be lost.

groups, it gets garbled and distorted. For instance, miners use mercury to process gold. The mercury is toxic and can kill fish, animals, and humans. When such information is passed along to remote villages, however, it becomes translated into different concepts because the Yanomami have no technical knowledge. To these people, mercury equals the bad magic enemy shamans blow at them to make them sick and die. This misinformation makes it harder for the Yanomami to combat the mercury problem and to avoid contaminated waterways.

Davi Kopenawa Yanomami

In spite of the cultural barriers, several Yanomami leaders have ventured out of their forest homes to address national audiences about their plight. Yanomami tribesman Davi Kopenawa Yanomami was nine years old the first time he and his people in Brazil saw a white man. The natives were so afraid that his mother hid him under a basket to protect him from the invaders—a group of geologists.

Nearly thirty years later, Davi's lands were under siege by gold panners in quest of mineral wealth. By that time, Davi had become an educated shaman and a leader of his people. This brought him to New York City in 1992, where he addressed the United Nations in a speech that helped begin the International Year of the World's Indigenous People.

While Davi was in New York he was shown around by author Geoffrey O'Connor. For the Yanomami shaman, simply crossing a street or traveling on a subway was a new and unusual experience. During the course of three weeks, Davi appeared on NBC's *Today* show and the CBS Evening News. He lectured at the Museum of Natural History and met with the head of the United Nations Human Rights Commission. Davi also traveled to Washington, D.C., where he spoke before a packed press conference before meeting with several influential senators and congressmen.

After nearly a month in the United States, Davi returned to his village, exhausted and anxious to see his family. When Brazil's new president, Fernando Collor de Mello, arrived in the United States a few weeks later, he did

Davi Kopenawa Yanomami (seated center) traveled to the United States in 1992, where he spoke about the plight of his Yanomami people.

not realize he was following in the wake of Davi, the now-famous Yanomami. Everywhere the president went he was confronted by questions about the Yanomami tragedy and the ongoing presence of tens of thousands of gold miners in their homeland. When he returned home, the president ordered the police to evict the gold miners and to blow up one hundred airstrips used by the miners.

According to an article in the March 1993 edition of *Progressive* magazine,

> For years, the Brazilian government turned a deaf ear to the Yanomami's pleas to have their lands protected. But . . . then-president of Brazil Fernando Collor de Mello bowed to international pressure and announced the creation of a single, continuous reserve for the remaining 9,000 Yanomami in Brazil. (There are also

roughly 12,000 Yanomami in Venezuela.) Collor also ordered the eviction of thousands of gold panners from the Yanomami lands. In May 1992, shortly before the Earth Summit in Rio de Janeiro, Collor finally ratified the measure calling for the demarcation of the reserve. . . .

The Yanomami say they are still waiting to receive their copy of the government documents proving that their land has been reserved. And the garimpeiros (gold miners) are back; to date, 8,000 or so have returned. Davi says he'll continue to fight until he rids the Yanomami of these invaders and forces the government to make good on its promises. Having spent ten years working for Funai, the government agency that oversees Indian affairs (but has done little for the Yanomami), Davi says he knows only too well that the government can't be trusted to live up to its end of the bargain.

"We've got to keep the pressure on," he says. "When we drive them crazy, that's when the authorities will do something."[34]

Medicines from the Jungle

While protecting Yanomami lands is imperative to their survival, certain efforts may help increase the value of ancient Yanomami knowledge. This is particularly true in the area of plant genetics and plant-based medicines.

Prescription medicines are one hallmark of modern civilization. They have cured or relieved pain from dozens of diseases that have haunted humankind for centuries. Ironically, the basis of a full 25 percent of these modern miracle drugs came from the primitive depths of the world's rain forests. Among these medicines are hydrocortisone, used to treat inflammation; reserpine for nervous disorders; vincristine for leukemia; digitalis for heart failure; quinine for malaria; and ipecac, which causes vomiting in the case of poisoning.

The rain forest has also provided drugs that show promise in treating cancer, sickle-cell anemia, herpes, Parkinson's disease, hypertension, and heart disease. Tribes in Amazonia have shown scientists 268 kinds of plants that can be used for human birth control alone. Richard Evans Schultes of Harvard University has been shown over 1,300 plant species that Indians of the Amazon use as medicines, poisons, or narcotics.

Drug companies profit by about $43 billion annually on prescription and nonprescription drugs that contain active ingredients derived from rain forests. Yet of an estimated 250,000 species of higher plants on earth, only about 5,000—or just 2 percent—have

yet been screened for medicinal properties. And there are perhaps 80,000 species of higher plants and 30 million animal species in Amazonia alone. Of the 3,000 species of plants that have been identified as having anticancer properties by the U.S. National Cancer Institute, 70 percent are from rain forests. Officials at the institute have said that destroying the rain forest would cause a major setback in the search for anticancer drugs.

Author Mark J. Plotkin is an ethnobotanist—a scientist who studies the use of plants by tribal peoples. In his book *Tales of a Shaman's Apprentice*, he talks about gathering

A Matses Indian holds medicinal plants to his stomach. Rain forest plants are an important source of drugs used in Western medicine.

medicinal plants with a Yanomami medicine man called the Jaguar Shaman:

> We stopped at a large liana, a woody vine that curved and twisted its way skyward through the bushes and small trees at the edge of the trail. The medicine man found a brown bean-shaped pod that had fallen from the vine. Breaking it open, he showed me the fruits, whose spherical shape and peculiar markings resembled little eyeballs. And sure enough, the . . . name for the plant, *tah-mo-ko ah-nu*, meant "howler monkey eye."

The medicine man indicated that he valued the sap of the liana's stem as a cure for children's fevers. Tah-mo-ko ah-nu is closely related to two other species from the legume family, which is rich in alkaloids. (Alkaloids are widely used for their sedative and muscle-relaxing effects. They include morphine and quinine.) These species play important roles in modern medicine. [A compound found in the plant] has been used by Western physicians since the 1950s to treat glaucoma, myasthenia gravis (weakness of the skeletal muscles, especially those of the face, neck, arms, and legs), and postpartum heartburn. And extracts of another species provides L-dopa, an amino acid in use since the late 1960s to treat Parkinson's disease. In the body, L-dopa is converted to dopamine, which facilitates nerve transmission in the brain.

The Jaguar Shaman taught me how to use the sap of the rubber tree to kill botfly larvae, how to use the exudate of the cotton plant to treat burns, and how to use the sap of edible palms to stanch the bleeding of severe cuts.[35]

In the early 1990s the wealth and diversity of healing plants in the jungle caught the attention of large international drug firms. Merck Pharmaceuticals has given million-dollar grants to South American countries to help develop new medicines from local plants. Bristol-Meyers-Squibb has negotiated with conservation groups to work with Amazonian Indians in search of new compounds. In addition, Eli Lilly is searching the jungle for new antifungal compounds from rain forest plants. These companies have also agreed to return a small portion of the profits to the native people.

In a related development, researchers are scouring the jungle for natural pesticides that can control insects that eat agricultural crops. Because there are so many species of insects in the rain forest, many plants have developed natural poisons to repel them. These natural chemicals have prompted researchers to find new types of insecticides that are less harmful to humans and the environment than synthetic chemicals now in widespread use.

Biosphere Reserves and Ecotourism

Some people who oppose mining and logging in the Amazon rain forest support a different kind of program to bring money to this region. Ecotourism is a type of travel that allows tourists to enjoy ecologically sensitive areas without causing them further damage. In the Amazon, tourists—mostly from the United States and Europe—get a chance to visit the rain forest and the Yanomami who live there. But even the most well-meaning program poses dangers to the tribal people.

Critics complain that ecotourism is supposed to be environment- and people-friendly, but it often treats indigenous people as exotic curiosities rather than people with full human

In 1980 the U.S. Supreme Court ruled that a company can own a patent and earn exclusive profits from a living organism. This started the modern biotechnology industry. Today, biotech and pharmaceutical companies are combing the Amazon rain forest looking for organisms and medicines that they can patent. This has set off a debate over who owns the rights to nature's healing plants. Author Noam Chomsky discusses the issue in the July/August 1992 issue of Z *Magazine:*

"Drug companies . . . [are] exploiting the accumulated knowledge of indigenous cultures for products that bring in some $100 billion profits annually, offering virtually nothing in return to the native people who lead researchers to the medicines, seeds, and other products they have developed and refined over thousands of years. 'The annual world market value for medicines derived from medicinal plants discovered from indigenous peoples is . . . $43 billion,' ethnobotanist Darrell Posey estimates. 'Less than 0.001 percent of the profits from drugs that originated from traditional medicine have ever gone to the indigenous people who led researchers to them.' Profits of at least the same scale derive from natural insecticides, insect repellents, and plant genetic materials, he believes. The international seed industry alone accounts for some $15 billion a year, based in large measure on genetic materials from crop varieties 'selected, nurtured, improved and developed by innovative Third World farmers for hundreds, even thousands of years,' Maria Elena Hurtado adds."

rights. And it treats tribal landholdings as if they were a wilderness theme park for visitors to explore. In some places Indians have even been driven off their land to make way for wildlife tourism.

Ecotourism can be beneficial to the Yanomami if certain guidelines and rules are followed. Some groups emphasize that the Indians are not "Stone Age people" but complex and ever-changing communities whose land ownership is recognized under international law. Land use for ecotourism, therefore, is subject to decisions made by the Yanomami themselves.

Ecotourism works better using another new idea—the concept of the biosphere reserve. The idea for this conservation area was first created by the United Nations Educational, Scientific, and Cultural Organization (UNESCO).

Biosphere reserves combine forest preservation with the needs of the human communities that live within the forests. The reserves have various zones, and each zone has different rules. One zone is the core, where natural vegetation and wildlife is permanently protected. The core zone is surrounded by rings of land used by human residents. These rings are called buffer zones. Local people may gather medicinal plants or harvest wild food from the first buffer zone, and scientists and tourists may enter to take photographs and collect specimens. In the next ring, local families farm and collect wood. The outer rings contain houses, hotels, and roads.

The plan would encourage tribal people to use the middle rings much as they have over the centuries. These families act as guardians of the buffer zones and the protected inner

Tourists purchase handmade goods from Amazon natives, part of a growing ecotourism movement.

core. It is crucial to the success of the biosphere reserve that local people plan and develop the area. Almost 250 biosphere reserves now exist in 65 countries. About one-fourth of these are in tropical rain forests.

Sustainable Development

Some ecologists want pristine land to be left untouched by human hands. But some in the Brazilian rain forest are promoting the idea that fragile ecosystems may best be preserved by allowing the indigenous people to live in and use them. This is called sustainable development. In a forest preserve about five hours west of the steamy Amazonian town of Tefe in northwestern Brazil, sustainable development is being practiced at an unprecedented level in an effort to save a little-studied ecosystem called the *varzea*.

The *varzea* is a species-rich area of the rain forest that is under water much of the year. During the seven-month-long wet season, these lowland areas are flooded up to thirty feet deep with river water. This is enough to submerge many low-growing plants and even tall trees. The plants and animals living there have had to make special adaptations to live in this watery environment.

In the 6,820-square-mile Mamiraua Ecological Station near the Upper Amazon, local people, called *caboclos*, were employed in 1993 as park rangers and researchers in a study to develop a *varzea* management plan. The project had lofty goals of creating a model for saving other endangered rain forests.

Some of the goals of the project, however, have generated controversy. When the preserve was declared, some ecologists wanted the *caboclos* moved out in accordance with a

Brazilian law that forbids settlements in parks and preserves. But instead, the project has been working to turn these peasants into game wardens and permanent caretakers, a tactic that has not always met with approval from rain forest researchers who believe that locals make poor land managers. But the Brazilian government has little money to employ rangers to enforce park laws (with an average of one ranger per 227,000 square miles of protected area). Those who support the project argue that the locals have a self-interest in maintaining the ecosystem that has supported them for so long. According to journalist Brian Alexander's article "People of the Amazon Fight to Save the Flooded Forest," in *Science* magazine,

So far, the gamble seems to be paying off. Most caboclos seem pleased by their new status, even though it means that certain forest zones are now off-limits to their use. "We are in a privileged situation," says one village leader. "We are lucky to be able to live here, to stay now that this is a preserve." One reason for their contentment may be that they have been given valuable incentives to compensate them for the restrictions they now face.

Communities have been given aid subsidies, for example, and almost all manual labor used by the project comes from the villages in the preserve. In particular, the project has been careful to select village

Young People Work to Save a Park

One example of environmental protection utilizing local inhabitants is the Piraja Memorial Project in Salvador, Brazil. The project has two goals: to affirm cultural identity and to protect the environment. The Piraja Metropolitan Park is a 155,000-acre forest reserve that is surrounded by overcrowded shantytowns where living conditions are marked by malnutrition, cholera, crime, and high infant mortality. Young people are exposed to violence, racism, and drugs, and the school dropout rate is very high. The park is under serious assault. The wildlife is hunted down, the plant life is devastated, the rivers are polluted by refuse, and forest fires are frequent.

In 1991 the Piraja Memorial Project selected a number of local young people aged fourteen to eighteen, to work as guides, make contact with other young people, and act as outreach agents in schools and in the community at large. Twenty-six teachers and seven hundred students were then recruited to replant and restore the site. In 1995 an environmental education program was started, offering students a chance to take part in practical activities, including school vegetable gardens. A library was also opened on the site.

After seeing the successful work that was done in the Piraja Metropolitan Park, UNESCO decided to make it an experimental zone of the Mata Atlantica Biosphere Reserve, also based in the area.

In 1996 the project published its own newspaper, staged a play about the park, employed artists to work for the park's cause, and set up workshops for children. The activities mobilized public opinion in favor of the project. Further plans for the park include an open-air museum to encourage the local population to learn more about nature and to respect it.

leaders and sons of leaders as employees. And income-generating experiments, the traditional way sustainable development works, are being tried. These include pilot projects to grow . . . fruit-bearing trees with commercial potential, and a census of the discus fish is being taken to determine if it can be culled for the aquarium trade. And Marmontel, who spends much of her time in the preserve and works closely with the caboclos, believes there are signs that the plan to use them as guardians against illegal fishing and logging is working. She has noted marked declines in both activities despite threats and some confrontations from armed gunmen on fishing boats and in logging camps. When the caboclos find an offender, they usually try friendly persuasion, but if the loggers or fishers refuse to leave, the caboclos report them to the project, which in turn calls in a federal ranger.[36]

The managers of Project Mamiraua hope to use information gathered there for a model in other areas of the rain forest.

Recording Native Music

Although sustainable development, ecotourism, and rain forest medicines hold monetary promise for the Amazon natives, there are other ways for the natives to earn money and to share their culture with the world.

The Brazilian tribe called the Suya live in central Brazil along the Suya-Missu River. Anthropologist Tony Seeger has been observing the traditional lifestyles of the Suya since 1971. Although they may once have numbered in the thousands, only 180 Suya live today—all of them in Lik-ko, the concentric village on the riverbank in the Mato Grosso.

Seeger was the first anthropologist to establish the importance of song and dance to the Suya, and today fifty-year-old Seeger is the curator of the Folkways Collection and the director of Folkways Recordings at the Smithsonian Institution. (Seeger comes from a musical family; Pete Seeger, his uncle, is a world-famous folk musician who gained popularity in the 1950s and 1960s.) One of the mandates of Folkways Recordings is to document the disappearing music and dance of ethnic minorities throughout the world. Folkways has issued a recording of Suya music, and Seeger's program enables the Suya to videotape and record their dances.

According to author David Roberts in *Smithsonian* magazine,

[Tribal leader] Tewensoti got to his feet to resume the Dance of the Hummingbirds. He took his place with more than 30 men and boys; trailing them came some 15 women, naked except for body paint, necklaces and waistbands of bright-colored beads. (When the Suya have a ceremony, they take off their clothing and paint their bodies because it is considered much more beautiful.)

The men set off, singing as they jogged, toward Tewensoti's house. Inside the dwelling the male dancers formed a large circle. Behind them stood the women. Like virtually all Suya dances, the Dance of the Hummingbirds was built around the repeated heavy stomp of the men's right feet, which laid down a solid 2:4 tempo. The only instrument was a gourd rattle. The singing was like nothing I had ever heard. A low-voiced unison dirge, ranging among only four or five notes but subtly syncopated with attacks that anticipated the beat, formed its foundation.

Sustainable Farming Development

Other programs to ensure the survival of the Amazon rain forest involves sustainable commercial farming. These programs work to find farming systems that can produce crops without destroying the forest; thus, their aim is to improve crop yields and farmers' incomes while conserving the natural environment.

This type of farming is called agroforestry, and it is based on ancient Yanomami farming techniques. An Amazon farmer, for example, would plant food crops as he or she normally would in jungle agriculture—but the farmer also plants tree crops such as rubber, cacao, coffee, citrus, or nuts on the same plot. By the time the food is harvested, the trees have grown enough to protect the soil from erosion and loss of nutrients. Then, the area beneath the tree crops is planted with crops that can tolerate shade. Later, the plot is given over totally to the tree crops. Years later, the farmer may cut down the trees for firewood or timber production. Eventually the plot can be replanted with food crops, and the cycle begins anew.

Agroforestry allows farmers to continually utilize a forest plot rather than just for two or three years. This, in turn, allows more land to remain in its natural state, which leaves a larger unaffected environment for the native people.

Above that, shrill cries—hawks' keenings, to my ears, rather than the trills of hummingbirds—flew antiphonally across the dark indoors.

One man in the middle of the jogging column stuck out incongruously, a head taller than anyone else, his pale white skin clashing with the olive hues around him. Over the years, Tony Seeger had learned the Dance of the Hummingbirds well enough to be invited to perform it. The chief's women had painted Tony's legs and torso, teasing him for his hairy chest (to the Suya, body hair is repellent, more appropriate to monkeys than to men). He let the men adorn him with a palm crown, and leg and arm wraps. Now he looked exhausted, though he gamely kept singing and stomping.[37]

Seeger records the Suya with a VCR powered by solar-charged batteries. Over the years, Seeger's commercial recordings of Suya songs have brought the people modest royalties since Folkways makes no profit from such discs. Still, what little money is made by the Suya helps them to survive in a changing world. When asked what he thought the biggest threat to the Suya was, surprisingly Seeger did not answer ranchers or gold miners.

"The encouragement of individualism," he said, "as opposed to the collective tribal good. I'm already seeing signs of it. Our rice and beans and coffee, for instance, weren't shared much beyond the chief's family, as they would have been in the 1970s."[38]

Projects like Seeger's bring to the world the beauty and culture of the forest's indigenous people. Coupled with other programs that combine native plant knowledge, ecology-friendly tourists, and unique farming techniques, survival of the Amazon's indigenous tribes may be assured in an ever-changing world.

The Amazon in the Twenty-First Century

The manners and customs of the Yanomami may seem strange to people in the "civilized" world, but at one time all humans probably lived like those in Amazonia. Like the Yanomami, the distant ancestors of today's civilized humans learned intimate details about their natural environment and exploited it to the best of their ability. What started as plant-based healing grew into modern medicine. What started as a talent to use handmade bows and arrows eventually took astronauts to the moon. Through the Yanomami we can gaze back twenty thousand years to the way all humankind once lived. But the Yanomami are more than a living museum, they are a sovereign people with as much right to exist in their own manner as the rest of humankind.

Until the mid-1990s the Yanomami people were the largest group of native Amazonians still living in isolation in the jungles of Brazil. Almost ten thousand of them inhabited 125 villages, spread throughout a fifty-eight-thousand-square-mile region near the border of Venezuela. According to anthropologists in Brazil, these indigenous people will become extinct in the next decade if the Brazilian government does not move to protect them. Malaria and other diseases are killing the Yanomami at a rate of 13 percent per year, and the birthrate hovers near zero. Young people who do survive are leaving the *shabonos*; only the old and the sick are to be found in some villages.

Although a growing number of ideas, plans, and schemes exists to save the Yanomami and their environment, there are just as many plans to exploit the forest and forever change the natural environment. The most recent plan to profit from the Amazon basin is to tap into the mighty tributaries of the river to generate electricity with a series of hydroelectric dams. The electricity would be used to extract minerals from such power-needy processes as mining bauxite. Lock gates with the dams, plus huge reservoirs, would allow big ships to approach the mineral sites to take away ore. Author Anthony Smith explains the scenario in his book *Explorers of the Amazon:*

These dams would therefore provide the power *and* the means for a further round of exploitation. Many observers believe that these major schemes are designed by and for the mega-rich with the aim of making them mega-mega-rich. . . .

Once again enormous tracts of forest will disappear, but everyone seems to have a reason for cutting down the trees. The big ranchers remove great swaths, so do the squatters, who work on a smaller scale but are more numerous. Every aspect of invasion, whether military or civil, unplanned villages or well-planned towns, is partnered by tremendous felling of trees as if trees are anathema (hated). Perhaps they are. Perhaps, however much lip-service is paid towards forest conservation, people in general dislike great tracts of trees, their darkness, their damp, their

Traditional ways of life disappear as disease and outside influences change Yanomami culture.

obscuring clear blue sky. The Indians make the place their home. For them there is no other way. Modern Amazonians favour a different form of life, and the forest is no part of it.[39]

As Smith points out, the United States finally realized the benefits of its own wilderness when only 5 percent of the original old-growth trees (such as California's giant sequoias) were left. Optimists in the Amazon expect no more than 10 percent of the trees to be left standing when the majority of South Americans begin to realize their own loss.

Perhaps Venezuelan anthropologist Jesús Cardozo summed it up best when he asked, "What will the future hold for the Yanomami? They desire so many things that we take for granted. Who can blame them? We can't keep them like a human museum."[40]

A Closing Message from Davi Kopenawa Yanomami

Outsiders may talk about the Yanomami and their forest home, but perhaps no one can speak better for the natives than Davi

Will the home of the Yanomami survive the encroachments of outsiders? Or will so-called "civilization" spoil all that is left of this paradise?

Kopenawa Yanomami. Here are the words of the Yanomami shaman, as posted on the Internet by the South and Meso American Indian Rights Center:

TO ALL WHO WISH TO HEAR ME

The biggest problem for the Yanomami now are the garimpeiro (goldminers) who are in our land, and the illnesses they bring with them. The government's National Health Foundation say that 1300 Yanomami had got malaria up until May this year. They have counted 24 airstrips opened by garimpeiros in the forest and they said that over 2500 men have illegally entered our reserve to pan for gold.

This information was published in the newspaper Folha de Boa Vista in May, you can see for yourselves.

Among them some have illnesses like flu, TB and venereal diseases, and contaminate my people. Now we are afraid they will bring measles and also AIDS, this illness which is so dangerous that we do not want it among us. But the worst illness for us is malaria, which comes in with the goldminers.

It is the Indians who keep the forest alive, because the Indians do not destroy nature looking for gold. The Indians do not spoil nature because they know it is important for the salvation of the planet Earth.

This is why we want the help of all those who understand that we only want to live in peace. If they do not help us, the garimpeiros will spoil all the rivers and leave us without fish or drinking water or game, destroying the health of the indians, the whites and the planet.

When I go to the big city I see people who are hungry, without anywhere to plant, without drinking water, without anywhere to live. I do not want this to happen to my people too, I do not want the forest to be destroyed, which leads to misery.

I am not saying that I am against progress. I think it is very good when whites come to work amongst the Yanomami to teach reading and writing, how to breed bees, how to use medicinal plants, the right ways of protecting nature. These white people are very welcome in our land. This for us is progress.

What we do not want are the mining companies, which destroy the forest, and the garimpeiros, who bring so many diseases. These whites must respect our Yanomami land. The garimpeiros bring guns, alcohol, prostitution and destroy nature wherever they go. The machines spill oil into the rivers and kill the life existing in them and the people and animals who depend on them. For us, this is not progress.

We want progress without destruction. We want to study, to learn new ways of cultivating the land, living from its fruits. The Yanomami do not want to live from dealing with money, with gold, we are not prepared for this. We need time to learn.

This is what I wanted to say to the whites who will listen to me, so that they can understand what the Yanomami want. We do not want to live without trees, hunting, fish and clean water. If this happens misery will come to our people.

That is why I am here, defending my land and my people. I hope that you will help me in this fight.[41]

Notes

Introduction: The Threatened Natives of the Amazon

1. Nigel J. H. Smith, *The Enchanted Amazon Rain Forest*. Miami: University Press of Florida, 1996, p. 63.
2. Quoted in Julie Sloan Denslow and Christine Padoch, eds., *People of the Tropical Rainforest*. Berkeley and Los Angeles: University of California Press, 1988, p. 73.
3. Donovan Webster, "The Orinoco: Heart of Venezuela," *National Geographic*, April 1998, p. 11.

Chapter 1: A Village Under One Roof

4. Quoted in Denslow and Padoch, *People of the Tropical Rainforest*, p. 75.
5. Napoleon A. Chagnon, *Yanomamö: The Last Days of Eden*. New York: Harcourt Brace Jovanovich, 1992, p. 74.
6. Chagnon, *Yanomamö*, p. 144.
7. Chagnon, *Yanomamö*, p. 8.
8. Chagnon, *Yanomamö*, p. 24.

Chapter 2: Living on the Forest's Bounty

9. Chagnon, *Yanomamö*, p. 158.
10. Chagnon, *Yanomamö*, pp. 99–100.
11. Quoted in Denslow and Padoch, *People of the Tropical Rainforest*, p. 80.

Chapter 3: Living in the Spirit World

12. Chagnon, *Yanomamö*, pp. 118–19.
13. Quoted in Webster, "The Orinoco," p. 13.
14. Chagnon, *Yanomamö*, p. 119.

15. Quoted in Chagnon, *Yanomamö*, p. 133.
16. Chagnon, *Yanomamö*, p. 66.
17. Chagnon, *Yanomamö*, p. 189.
18. Chagnon, *Yanomamö*, p. 203.

Chapter 4: Late Arrivals

19. Chico Mendes, *Fight for the Forest*. London: Latin American Bureau (Research and Action), 1989, p. 17.
20. Quoted in Binka Le Breton, *Voices from the Amazon*. West Hartford, CT: Kumarian Press, 1993, p. 77.
21. Quoted in Le Breton, *Voices from the Amazon*, pp. 78–79.
22. Quoted in Le Breton, *Voices from the Amazon*, pp. 22–24.
23. Quoted in Geoffrey O'Connor, *Amazon Journal*. New York: Dutton, 1997, p. 40.
24. O'Connor, *Amazon Journal*, p. 29.
25. O'Connor, *Amazon Journal*, p. 66.
26. O'Connor, *Amazon Journal*, p. 70.

Chapter 5: Outside Influences

27. Chagnon, *Yanomamö*, p. 273.
28. Chagnon, *Yanomamö*, p. 273.
29. Quoted in Denslow and Padoch, *People of the Tropical Rainforest*, p. 91.
30. O'Connor, *Amazon Journal*, p. 44.
31. O'Connor, *Amazon Journal*, p. 140.

Chapter 6: Survival in a Changing World

32. Chagnon, *Yanomamö*, p. 277.
33. Quoted in Susanna Hecht and Alexander Cockburn, *The Fate of the Forest*. New York: Verso, 1989, p. 193.
34. L. A. Winokur, "Emissary from the Rain Forest," *Progressive*, March 1993, p. 14.

35. Mark J. Plotkin, *Tales of a Shaman's Apprentice*. New York: Viking, 1993, p. 97.
36. Brian Alexander, "People of the Amazon Fight to Save the Flooded Forest," *Science*, July 29, 1994, p. 607.
37. David Roberts, "The Suya Sing and Dance and Fight for a Culture in Peril," *Smithsonian*, May 1996, p. 64.
38. Roberts, "The Suya Sing and Dance and Fight for a Culture in Peril," p. 64.

Epilogue: The Amazon in the Twenty-First Century

39. Anthony Smith, *Explorers of the Amazon*. New York: Viking, 1990, p. 331.
40. Quoted in Webster, "The Orinoco," p. 11.
41. Quoted in the South and Meso American Indian Rights Center, available http://www.nativeweb.org/saiic.

For Further Reading

Books and Periodicals

Napoleon A. Chagnon, *Yanomamö: The Last Days of Eden*. New York: Harcourt Brace Jovanovich, 1992. Chagnon is a pioneering anthropologist and a world-famous expert on the Yanomami people. He has lived with them off and on since the 1960s, speaks their language, and has participated in their daily lives. Many other books about the Yanomami are based on this book, which is full of entertaining stories about the author's life among the Yanomami.

Julie Sloan Denslow and Christine Padoch, eds., *People of the Tropical Rainforest*. Berkeley and Los Angeles: University of California Press, 1988. Details the lives of indigenous people who live in the world's rain forests, including their traditional lifestyles and the problems caused by deforestation and encroaching civilization.

Theresa Greenaway, *Jungle*. New York: Alfred A. Knopf, 1994. A big, colorful Eyewitness Book full of photos and easy-to-read text detailing the intricate web of life in jungles across the globe.

Binka Le Breton, *Voices from the Amazon*. West Hartford, CT: Kumarian Press, 1993. This book documents the thoughts and actions of real people who work and live in Amazonia. Le Breton interviews Indians, loggers, river people, miners, settlers, ranchers, rubber tappers, and those trying to save the forest.

Rosemary McConnel, *The Amazon*. Morristown, NJ: Silver Burdett, 1978. A book for young adults that covers many aspects of life on the Amazon River, including sections on wildlife, early explorers, modern cities, natives, and habitat destruction.

Chico Mendes, *Fight for the Forest*. London: Latin American Bureau (Research and Action), 1989. A book written by the leader of the Brazilian rubber tappers' union. Mendes talks about his life's work fighting loggers in the Amazon and struggling to develop sustainable alternatives to development.

James D. Nations, *Tropical Rainforests*. New York: Franklin Watts, 1988. A straightforward, easy-to-read book that details the beauty of the Amazon rain forest and the threats it faces.

Geoffrey O'Connor, *Amazon Journal*. New York: Dutton, 1997. This book was written by a documentary filmmaker as he struggled against military orders to capture the Amazonian gold rush on film. It includes a blistering account of the forces of destruction at work against the Yanomami and their environment.

Mark J. Plotkin, *Tales of a Shaman's Apprentice*. New York: Viking, 1993. Plotkin is an ethnobotanist who recounts his travels and studies with powerful Amazonian shamans. He also details his race against the loggers to record new plants and learn their healing properties.

David M. Schwartz, *Yanomami, People of the Amazon*. New York: Lothrop, Lee & Shepard Books, 1995. This large book about the Yanomami is full of beautiful pictures and is written for young adults. It includes dozens of photographs of Yanomami at work, play, and spiritual pursuits.

Nigel J. H. Smith, *The Enchanted Amazon Rain Forest*. Miami: University Press of Florida, 1996. An enchanting book that weaves facts about Amazonia with folk tales and legends that are native to the region. The author compiled this book over twenty-five years.

Donovan Webster, "The Orinoco: Heart of Venezuela," *National Geographic*, April 1998. A beautiful article about life on the Orinoco River, covering the lands of the

Yanomami to the villages, towns, and cities that thrive from the river's bounty further downstream.

Organizations and Websites

Amanaka'a Amazon Network
60 E. 13th St., 5th Fl.
New York, NY 10003
(212) 253-9502
fax: (212) 253-9507
e-mail: amanakaa@amanakaa.org
web address: www.amanakaa.org/
Amanaka'a Amazon Network is a nonprofit environmental education organization with a simple mission: to support the peoples of the Amazon rain forest in their efforts to live and work in harmony with their environment.

Arawak Struggles in the Amazon
web address: www.hartford-hwp.com/taino/links1.html
Dedicated to the struggles of Arawak-speaking peoples of the Amazonian basin, this organization works to preserve their culture and livelihood.

Commission for the Creation of the Yanomami Park
Rua Manoel da Nobrega, 111 conj. 32
04001 São Paulo, SP—Brasil
011-5511-925-1200
fax: 011-5511-284-6997
The commission regularly publishes bulletins and alerts on the Yanomami situation.

Rainforest Action Network
450 Sansome, Suite 700
San Francisco, CA 94111
(415) 398-4404
fax: (415) 398-2732
e-mail: rainforest@igc.apc.org
web address: www.ran.org
The Rainforest Action Network works to protect the earth's rain forests and supports the rights of their inhabitants through education, grassroots organizing, and nonviolent direct action.

Rainforest Alliance Home Page
65 Bleecker St.
New York, NY 10012
(888) MY-EARTH (693-2784)
web address: www.rainforest-alliance.org/
The Rainforest Alliance is one of the largest organizations concerned with rain forests the world over.

Rainforest Foundation International
270 Lafayette, #1107
New York, NY 10012
(212) 431-9098
e-mail: rffny@rffny.org
web address: www.savetherest.org/foundation.html
This organization was founded by Trudie Styler and her rock-star husband, Sting. Its mission is to support indigenous peoples and traditional populations of the rain forest in their efforts to protect their environment by helping them secure and control their natural resources.

South and Meso American Indian Rights Center
PO Box 28703
Oakland, CA 94602
(510) 834-4263
e-mail: saiic@igc.apc.org
web address: http://www.nativeweb.org/saiic
The center publishes news and articles relating to indigenous issues in Central and South America.

Tropical Rainforest Coalition
461 Park Ave., Suite #4
San Jose, CA 95110
(408) 496-9412.
web address: www.rainforest.org/
The coalition is a children-oriented organization that helps protect the world's tropical rain forests.

Yanomami Survival Fund
PO Box 30426
Santa Barbara, CA 93105
Organized by anthropologist Napoleon A. Chagnon, the world's foremost expert on the Yanomami people, this organization distributes information about programs that support the Yanomami cause.

Works Consulted

Brian Alexander, "People of the Amazon Fight to Save the Flooded Forest," *Science*, July 29, 1994. An article about local people helping ecologists save a fragile ecosystem called the *varzea*, which is the flooded forest of Amazonia.

Noam Chomsky, "Year 50!: World Orders Old and New," Z *Magazine*, July/August 1992. An article about how U.S. biotech firms dominated the hunt for DNA and other genetic material in the world's rain forests.

Jacques Yves Cousteau, *Jacques Cousteau's Amazon Journey*. New York: Harry N. Abrams, 1984. A large book with many photographs by naturalist, filmmaker, and inventor of the aqualung, Jacques Cousteau. A very detailed and scientific account of his adventures sailing up the Amazon.

Art Davidson, *Endangered Peoples*. San Francisco: Sierra Club Books, 1993. An oversized book about endangered indigenous peoples all over the world, with a section about the Yanomami. Gives good perspective on the problems faced by natives in North America, Latin America, Africa, Asia, and the Pacific Islands.

Kenneth Good, "Amazon Grace," *Natural History*, March 1997. An article about the rituals and ordeals a young Yanomami man must go through in order to become a shaman.

Susanna Hecht and Alexander Cockburn, *The Fate of the Forest*. New York: Verso, 1989. A book about the people who have hurt the rain forest and those who have lived there and helped save it. Travels back in time to the early days of Amazonian exploitation and ends with the murder of Chico Mendes.

Kenton Miller and Laura Tangley, *Trees of Life*. Boston: Beacon Press, 1991. A hard-hitting book that offers suggestions to tropical nations for revamping their approaches to forestry, agriculture, population, and indigenous people. Includes information on destruction of the rain-forests in the Pacific Northwest region of the United States.

David Roberts, "The Suya Sing and Dance and Fight for a Culture in Peril," *Smithsonian*, May 1996. An article that details an anthropologist's travels as he records the songs and dances of the Suya tribe in the Brazilian rain forest.

Anthony Smith, *Explorers of the Amazon*. New York: Viking, 1990. Smith recounts the stories of men and women who were drawn to the interior of the Amazon jungle over the centuries, including Spanish conquistadors, eighteenth-century explorers, nineteenth-century naturalists, and more. This book is well researched and exciting to read.

L. A. Winokur, "Emissary from the Rain Forest," *Progressive*, March 1993. An article about tribal leader Davi Kopenawa Yanomami, who left the Amazon to travel to New York, and which describes the plight of his people to a UN conference on indigenous people.

Index

fishing, 28
Folkways Recordings, 82
food, 23, 26–27
  cooking, 28
  in feasts, 44
  planting, 28–30
  search for, 27–28, 31

gardens. *See* planting
Ge-speaking people, 11
gold mining, 12, 59–61
  politics influenced by, 69–71
  in Venezuela, 72–73
Good, Kenneth, 41
Goodyear, Charles, 52
Government Decree 1850, 72
grubs, 31
Guarani Indians, 71–72

hallucinogenic drugs, 29, 38,
  40–43
headman, 18
hekura (spirits), 40
Herodotus, 51
highways, 53–54
hisiomö tree, 41
honey, 27
human rights, 55
Humboldt, Alexander von, 49
hunting, 23, 27
Hurtado, Maria Elena, 79
hydrocortisone, 77
hydroelectric dams, 84

Indian Protection Service, 62
Indians. *See* natives; Yanomami In-
  dians
indigenous people. *See* natives;
  Yanomami Indians
International Year of the World's
  Indigenous People, 75
ipecac, 77
iron ore, 59
Iwäriwä (spirit of fire), 38

Jesuit missionaries, 49
José, king of Portugal, 52
Juca, Romero, 60

Karina tribe, 72

Kayapó Indians, 11, 67–68
kraiwa (foreigners), 62
Kuikuru tribe, 29

language, 11, 36
L-dopa, 78
Le Breton, Binka, 56
liana vine, 78
Lik-ko (village), 82
logging, 12, 57–59, 72

Mackintosh, Charles, 52
maize (corn), 26, 31
malaria, 64, 66, 70, 86
Malaysia, 50
Mamiraua Ecological Station, 80
Mamiraua Project, 80–82
mamukure plant, 29
manioc, 26, 28, 29
marriage, 21–22
  feasts and, 44
Mata Atlantica Biosphere Reserve,
  81
Mato Grosso do Sul, 69, 71, 82
measles, 66
medical care, 66
medicine, 76–78, 79
Mehinaku tribe, 11
men, Yanomami, 18–19, 21–22
  as shamans, 40, 41
Mendes, Chico, 51–52, 54, 57
Menkragnoti territory, 68
Merck Pharmaceuticals, 78
mercury, 72
mining, 59–61
  politics influenced by, 69–71
  in Venezuela, 72–73
missionaries, 49, 62–63
mokohiros (hollow tubes), 41
music, 82–83
myths, 38–39

name taboos, 24–25
nape (people), 36–38
National Geographic, 11–12,
  37–38
National Health Foundation, 86
natives, 8, 10–11
  efforts to help, 67–68
    through ecotourism, 78–80

through medicinal plants,
    77–78
  through music, 82–83
  through sustainable develop-
    ment, 80–82
highway development and, 54
land rights of, 68–69
  vs. commercial interests,
    69–72
  ignored, 72–73
  music of, 82–83
  rubber boom and, 50
  sold into slavery, 49
  in Venezuela, 72
  see also Yanomami Indians
Natural History, 41
natural resources, 59, 65, 72
  see also rubber tappers
New Tribes of Brazil, 62
no badabö (spirit/human), 38

O'Connor, Geoffrey, 60, 61, 65, 67,
  70
Operation Amazonia, 53–54
Opikteri Hamo, 64
Orellana, Francisco de, 51
Orinoco River, 11, 49, 59

Panoan people, 11
Pemon tribe, 72
People of the Tropical Rainforest
  (Caneiro), 14
Peru, 8–9
Piraja Memorial Project, 81
plantains, 26, 31, 44
planting, 28–30
  after moving, 30–31
  sustainable development and,
    83
  through slash-and-burn, 31–35
plants, healing, 77–78
Plotkin, Mark J., 77–78
politics, 69-71
Portugese, 49, 52
Posey, Darrell, 79
Progressive magazine, 76
Project Mamiraua, 80–82
prostitution, 68
Protestant Evangelical Amazonic
  Mission, 62

Picture Credits

About the Author

Stuart A. Kallen is the author of more than 140 nonfiction books for children and young adults. He has written on topics ranging from the theory of relativity to rock-and-roll history to life on the American frontier. In addition, Kallen has written award-winning children's videos and television scripts. In his spare time, Kallen is a singer/songwriter/guitarist in San Diego, California.